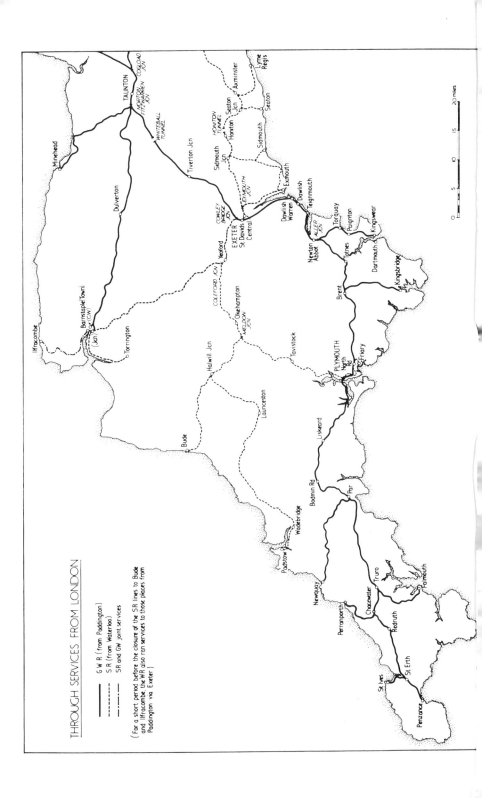

THROUGH SERVICES FROM LONDON

——————— G W R (from Paddington)
- - - - - - - S R (from Waterloo)
—·—·—·— SR and GW joint services

(For a short period before the closure of the SR lines to Bude
and Ilfracombe, the WR also ran services to those places from
Paddington via Exeter)

Summer Saturdays in the West

Summer Saturdays in the West

David St John Thomas
&
Simon Rocksborough Smith

with illustrations by
Peter Gray & Kenneth Leech

DAVID & CHARLES
Newton Abbot London North Pomfret (Vt)

ISBN 0 946537 04 6

First published 1973
Second impression 1978
Third impression 1983

Set in 11/13 Press Roman
and printed in Great Britain
by Redwood Burn Ltd, Trowbridge, Wilts.
for David St John Thomas
and distributed by David & Charles
Brunel House Newton Abbot Devon

Contents

		Page
Introduction		7
	PART ONE - THE GENERAL BACKGROUND	11

Chapter

I	The Historical Background	13
II	Portrait of the System in 1957	16
III	The Contrast with today	48
	Photographs	52

PART TWO - 1957	75

PART THREE - 1971	125

APPENDIX TABLE (Schedule showing progress of trains to and from West of England 27 July 1957)	139
Down Trains	142
Up Trains	159
Further Notes on 27 July 1957	173
Acknowledgements	174

List of Illustrations

		Page
Map		2

Photographs

1	*Eastbury Grange* at Whiteball Summit	52
2	*King Henry III*, Brewham bank	53
3	Kennet & Avon Canal at Savernake	54
4	Creech troughs	55
5	*Mursley Hall* at Whiteball	56
6	*Brocket Hall* at Whiteball	57
7	*King Richard I* at Whiteball	58
8	5341 at Whiteball	59
9	*Beaufort* at Taunton	60
10	*Manorbier Castle* at Exeter St David's	61
11	*King Henry III* and *Earl of Radnor* at Exeter St David's	62
12	*Squadron* and *King Edward VI* at Exeter St David's	63
13	Powderham, *The Devonian*	64
14	*St Fagans Castle* at Dawlish	65
15	Newton Abbot	66
16	Aller Junction	67
17	*Enville Hall* at Torre	68
18	3796 at Torquay	69
19	*Caradoc Grange* at Torquay	70
20	Rattery Bank	71
21	Wrangaton	72
22	*Saighton Grange* at Doublebois	73

Introduction

This is a work of joint authorship. So far as I am concerned it had its beginnings when Peter Gray, one of the really outstanding photographers of the last days of Western steam, asked if David & Charles would be interested in a work illustrated by him and written by Simon Rocksborough Smith, on the working of the Western Region's main line on 27 July 1957, the busiest day in the history of West Country railways when the number of passengers carried was probably twice what it will ever be again.

Peter Gray wrote in his introductory letter that he doubted if David & Charles would find the project economic, but that though he knew 'business and sentiment do not mix' I might be interested in view of my strong personal connection with summer Saturday operations. Well, it is a specialised subject, and yet at the same time it was a very important one, and certainly the events of 27 July 1957 involved a large proportion of the West Country's population. And in the case of David & Charles business and sentiment are not totally divorced: how could they be when my publishing office is on Newton Abbot station in the very rooms occupied by the Motive Power Department who organised the fight to keep the wheels moving that and other busy Saturdays?

Interesting however though the close-up on the single Saturday is, it seemed to me that we also needed a more general portrayal of what happened on western rails on summer Saturdays as a whole, and indeed I had lived and breathed summer Saturdays so deeply over many years that occasionally the thought had already struck me that the subject would make an interesting and unusual book.

So I have written the general background, Simon Rocksborough Smith deals with the specific day — and includes his own introduction to that — while many of the illustrations come from Peter Gray. None of us would claim we have produced a piece of literature but we have I think done something to catch the atmosphere of a colourful era when the railways brought the majority of visitors and still relied on steam power to do so.

Empress of Canada, 1971   David St John Thomas

Notes from the introduction to the 1978 edition

Many extra trains continue to run from Paddington (including through trains to Barnstaple and, after a break of several years, on the Falmouth branch) and from various Midland and North Country starting points. Certain traditions continue: extra trains from Liverpool, Leeds and Newcastle arrive with 12 or 13 of the oldest coaches, though now many London trains are composed of Mark II air-conditioned stock and one is very conscious when glancing at passengers crowded in second-class compartments that such older stock will not be around much longer.

There is no longer a decline in traffic: the railways have found their niche, helped by marketing devices such as Golden Rail to the chief resorts. Although Saturday journey times from London are much the same as in 1971, many cross-country trains have been speeded up; for instance, it takes three quarters of an hour less to reach Penzance from Manchester or Bradford.

Familiar features such as trains being halted at Dawlish (the signal box is now only open on summer Saturdays) continue. With the withdrawal of all the Western Region's diesel hydraulic locomotives and the abolition of identification head codes even on summer Saturdays, part of the interest has inevitably gone, but High Speed Train sets on the London route will soon add a touch of variety of their own. And also for variety on summer Saturdays the Torbay Steam Railway provides genuine connections for long-distance passengers at Paignton, so once more you can end your journey in a chocolate-and-cream train hauled by a green locomotive.

Introduction to the 1983 edition

The interest in summer Saturdays, past and present, is maintained, and it is gratifying to note that this book (which, to most people, seemed extraordinarily specialised when first written twelve years ago) remains in steady demand. We mainly tell of the way the railways strained themselves to convey armies of peacetime holiday-makers like a military operation in the last days that trains carried over half the visitors going to the West Country. But here let us take the opportunity briefly to up-date the picture.

The timetable for the main line and most branches is still recast in total for summer Saturdays, and at peak times (especially at the end of July and beginning of August when there are still a few unadvertised relief services) trains pass along the Sea Wall between Dawlish and Teignmouth with almost incredible frequency – and at much higher speeds than even in 1971. But in 1983 only two branches – Paignton and Newquay – were served with through trains from Paddington and the cross-country route via Birmingham. The withdrawal of the Paddington to Barnstaple service, which used to reverse at Exeter St David's was surprising. But a morning train ran from Barnstaple to Waterloo, no doubt raising many ghosts along the traditional route of Southern trains like the Atlantic Coast Express. And there was still a reversal off former Southern to Western metals at St David's with the extension of the Brighton service to Paignton.

Of the 'traditionals', Dawlish signalbox still opened on summer Saturdays, and some Liverpool and Manchester trains used the North-to-West route via Shrewsbury and the Severn Tunnel. Extra trains of up to twelve of the now-oldest (Mark I) coaches continued to arrive from Liverpool, Leeds and Newcastle, but thirteen-coach trains have become rare. Innovations included an Aberdeen section on a Glasgow train. The decline in the number of trains since 1971 is perhaps less than one might expect.

The dramatic change has been in speed. By 1983 High Speed Trains formed all regular daytime services on Saturdays between Paddington and Plymouth or Penzance, and a few between Paddington and Paignton. HSTs also accounted for some of the cross-country services to/from Leeds, Bradford, Newcastle and Edinburgh.

Regular main-line express passenger trains calling at or passing through Exeter on Summer Saturdays:

		1971	*1977*	*1982*
Down trains	00.00 – 07.00	18	14	12
Down trains	09.30 – 18.30	43	41	36
Up trains	08.30 – 19.30	53	51	49

Comparative journey time Newcastle-Paignton:

	Dep Newcastle	Arr Paignton	Hours	Minutes
1957 Steam	07.30	18.13	10	43
1971 Diesel	07.26	16.25	8	59
1977 Diesel	09.03	17.28	8	25
1982 HST	07.30	14.27	6	57

Indeed, so far from providing the touch of variety hinted at in the introduction to the 1978 edition, the HSTs have become almost monotonous.

The four Motorail trains of summer Saturdays in 1977 had declined to two in 1982: from Stirling (overnight) and Paddington (cars only, the passengers now travelling by ordinary train). After many years of compulsory seat reservation (or 'Regulation') on the peak Saturdays, in 1982 the reserving of seats was in theory 'advisory' only, though only those with reservations were admitted to certain services. Banking engines have long disappeared on the Torbay branch, but even in 1978 nobody could have foretold that by 1982 the depot they operated from – Newton Abbot – would be totally closed. Newton's huge expanse of carriage sidings also lay empty, soon to be taken up, while on Saturday afternoons and evenings a succession of empty trains from the Torbay branch worked either to Plymouth, or up the main line to places as far afield as Nottingham and Wolverhampton, for stabling.

Though long-distance passenger traffic has remained remarkably stable, ever less of the Great Western's character shows through. Next to go are the lower quadrant signals and all signalboxes between Exeter and Plymouth. Many signals have already been removed. As a boy I could see eight signal arms, controlled by three signalboxes, along the Sea Wall at Teignmouth. Now there is just one quadrant home and electric light distant on the down line, nothing on the up at all. Even the evening milk trains, which had to be fitted in whatever the pressure, are but a memory.

See page 174 for corrections to the information regarding 1957.

January 1983   David St John Thomas

PART ONE

The General Background

CHAPTER I

The Historical Background

The West Country's tourist industry owes almost everything to the railways. The resorts which developed quickest and most solidly around groups of large hotels were those first served by trains; to this day there is not a single well-balanced resort (with large hotels as well as cheaper forms of accommodation) that did not once have its own station. Even in relatively undeveloped areas like North Devon, the railways set the pattern which road traffic still largely follows now that most of the rails have been taken up.

At the beginning most West Country watering places, notably Exmouth, Dawlish, Teignmouth and Torquay, the first to be reached by trains, concentrated on the winter season, boasting of the mildness of their climate and the range of their entertainment and social facilities (such as Teignmouth's famous Carlton Club, now the Riviera Cinema). As late as the 1890s, when following the abandonment of Brunel's broad gauge, the first through trains ran from the North to Torbay, the resorts were still busier in winter than in summer, when many of their facilities closed down. Sea bathing (of course dependent on the bathing machine) was however growing rapidly in popularity and certainly local traffic was heavier in summer; Exeter in particular has a strong tradition of sending its people to the sea on day trips, 5,000 or more leaving the city on Saturday mornings in the Augusts of the later 1890s. And by 1914 the upper middle class family holiday by the sea was more usually a summer affair, brass bands playing through August and September and changing their recess to winter or late spring. An indication of what lay ahead was the *Devon and Cornwall Special,* a third-class-only restaurant car train (unthinkable only a decade before on the GWR) from Paddington to Torquay and

Paignton, Newquay and Falmouth. In 1913 its up journeys operated every Saturday in August and September. Going down it made
journeys on Thursday, Friday and Saturday, 31 July and 1 and 2
August (the Bank Holiday weekend peak was just establishing
itself) and then ran Saturdays only till 20 September. It was slightly ahead of its time and did not do as well as expected.

The First War was followed by dramatic changes; after it a
sharply rising proportion of the middle class took an annual two-
to-eight weeks by the sea, often still travelling with servants and
even portable bath, 'taking' a house and using the railway as much
for local travel during their stay as for the journey from city to
resort. The honeymoon business, too, became substantial, materi-
ally adding to the summer demand for hotel accommodation. Often
the honeymoon set the pattern for a yearly hotel holiday thereafter,
many hotels accepting their first babies and young children at this
time.

By the mid-1920s traffic from Paddington was much heavier on
summer Saturdays than at any other time and the first of the
summer Saturday-only holiday expresses, such as the *Kingsbridge
and Newquay Express,* had made their appearance on the timetable.
At first such trains tended to operate only for four or six weeks at
the season's peak, but by the mid-1930s, when Monday-to-Friday
and Saturday schedules were printed separately in the timetable
for the first time, many of the holiday expresses stretched from
June to September with others operating shorter periods. This in
many ways was the gilt on the Great Western's golden age. The
GWR as a whole was enjoying new-found confidence and with its
'Books for Boys of All Ages', its jig-saw puzzles, enterprising
restaurant-car menus and other devices encouraging travellers to
regard the journey as one of the most enjoyable parts of their
holiday. Such was the increase in traffic presenting itself for the
long Saturday journey to Devon and Cornwall, at a time when
business generally was not so booming for Britain's railways, that
very high priority was given to increasing facilities.

Paddington was largely rebuilt with the Saturday peaks of West
Country traffic in mind. Taunton station, which had proved a terri-
ble bottleneck at the end of the 1920s, was spaciously rebuilt and
the four miles of track from Cogload Junction to Norton
Fitzwarren quadrupled, again largely to cope with the summer

Saturday traffic in the early 1930s. It was incidentally as the result of the quadrupling through Taunton (and the increased flexibility that gave) that train reporting had to be introduced so that stations further west knew which trains were coming in which order. Each train was given a number which was carried on the front of locomotives.

Further west Newton Abbot was rebuilt in 1927, and a number of main line stations were quadrupled (the platforms being served by loops) in the 1930s. There was a grandiose scheme not finally abandoned till after the Second War to bypass Dawlish and Teignmouth by an inland cut-off. New crossing loops were installed on the Minehead branch and extra signalboxes between Exeter and Teignmouth just to cope with the peak demand on eight or nine Saturdays a year, and destination boards were freely commissioned for some of the expresses running only on those days.

Each season brought new advertised trains and unadvertised duplicates, but it was very much a case of adding something extra and adapting a bit each season, there never being any major recast or even policy review as the traffic doubled, trebled and quadrupled. When war came again, most of the holiday expresses disappeared but some that ran still did so to the pre-war pattern; and after 1945 it was again a case of continuity with piecemeal adaptation.

CHAPTER II

Portrait of the System in 1957

In the years immediately after the end of World War II, when the West Country emerged as Britain's foremost tourist area, an ever-greater number of visitors had to be moved by train. Well into the 1950s over half the total visitors, at least in the peak weeks, came by the railways whose resources were stretched to breaking point, and sometimes beyond.

The major problem was that ever more people came during a few hectic weeks in July and August and that most of them travelled on Saturdays. Indeed it was only after the majority of visitors switched to private car transport in the later 1950s and early 1960s that at last the season began to be staggered or lengthened – for while train passengers were content merely to grumble about delays on the rail on peak days, many car drivers were unprepared to repeat queueing for hours on end in the blazing sun. One of the tragedies of the situation from the railways' point of view was that they *could* manage to meet the peak demand in the way that later the road system could not, but the standard of service was often atrociously poor. Many passengers alas only experienced train travel in these unhappiest of conditions and this must have encouraged many to hasten buying cars.

While the railway remained the number one carrier of visitors, there was likewise no real movement to stagger travel within the holiday week. Especially at the season's peak well over nine out of ten visitors arrived and departed on Saturdays and in a period when hotel and especially camping accommodation was generally scarce it was generally only possible to book Saturday to Saturday in the resorts. Again it was the rise of private car traffic and congestion on the roads that forced some degree of staggering the holiday week. People who had been prepared to suffer a Saturday train journey extended by, say, two hours over Monday to Friday schedules were not, once they became car owners, willing to sit at the wheel up to three times as long as in mid week.

It was thus the railway system's very elasticity, its capability of handling twenty times as many people on summer Saturdays than on other days, that tended to be self-defeating. Over the years many millions of Britons suffered a worse quality of train travel than they would have enjoyed had the season been only moderately lengthened and the travel week only a little staggered. But at that time the railways served both the resorts and the public as they wished to be served, and quite heroic efforts were indeed made to move the ever greater number of summer Saturday passengers.

As has already been stated it was as long ago as the late 1920s that the Great Western Railway first evolved different schedules for the greater number of summer Saturday passengers, and in the 1930s over twice as many passengers used the Taunton-Newton Abbot stretch on summer Saturdays as on other days. Even during World War II there were some extra trains on July and August Saturdays. But it was from 1945 on, with the advent of holidays with pay for the masses, that traffic reached gargantuan proportions. The printed timetables for those years by no means tell the full story for many trains ran in up to five parts, though steadily more services were advertised year by year reaching a peak in the late 1950s, in fact after traffic had started to decline, so that travelling conditions improved. There was however always the question whether it was better to provide more trains on the peak days and thus risk total congestion and increased delays (but with all passengers theoretically comfortably seated) or whether the number of trains should be limited in the interest of keeping the majority moving smoothly.

The whole problem of moving these armies of holidaymakers on the half dozen busiest Saturdays each year was tackled like a military operation with growing understanding and sophistication. During the whole of this period I was not merely a railway enthusiast living near the railway at Newton Abbot but a journalist, including being Holiday Correspondent to the West Country's regional daily *The Western Morning News* and also covering the subject (often the front page lead) for the Sunday *Independent.*

I described the Saturday's battles to move the crowds as sports critics cover football matches and indeed the subject was of burning interest since on any one Saturday not only would up to half a million passengers be involved but how well the trains ran would affect the work, life and reputations of thousands of people like taxi drivers, hotel and camp keepers and not least the railwaymen themselves. How well the trains ran was a subject of universal interest in a way it will never be again outside the London commuter zone.

Quite apart from the practical importance of the railway system, however, there was the pure interest in theoretically getting the most out of the system: it's always fun to see something (even the parking areas around our homes) used to its maximum capacity and beyond. And then there were the trains themselves – long trains often composed of motley assortments of ancient carriages (vehicles that would have been scrapped before I was old enough to appreciate them had they not been retained especially for the peak Saturday working) hauled by freight engines and almost anything that would move, as well as the 'Castles' and 'Kings', the last of the 'Saints' and the new 'Counties'.

Summer Saturdays in the west. The subject is so diverse and so colourful that it's hard to know where to begin. A memory I shall certainly always retain was the change in mood on those overcrowded trains especially from the North in the years immediately after the war when the sea was reached at Dawlish Warren. Many thousands of children caught their first glimpse of the waves there and all the delays and grumbles were forgotten – indeed there was positive disappointment if the train weren't slowed down by signals between here and Teignmouth.

Parson's Tunnel between Dawlish and Teignmouth was one of a number of signalboxes controlling no points that were opened on summer Saturdays especially to shorten sections on the Taunton-Newton Abbot portion of the route, the most intensively used. The common experience of westward bound travellers whether from London or the North or Midlands via Bristol was to enjoy a fairly smooth journey to Taunton, where of course the London and Bristol lines converge. From there on, on the busiest days it could be a question of dawdling from one signalbox to another: trains from the two routes simply arrived at Taunton more rapidly than they could be sent on. In theory of course there should never have been delays and just occasionally things did go like clockwork, every train keeping its scheduled passage. But it needed only one minor delay to waste some track occupation between Taunton and Newton Abbot and many following trains would be affected. And since trains came from all over the country, carried up to 1,000 passengers a piece, stopped at station platforms already swarming with humanity, and were often under-powered, delays of one kind or another were to be assumed. More often than not trains arrived at Taunton out of timetable order.

Even telling which train was what was one of the hazards of summer Saturday working. The timetables and the weekly working instructions setting out details of extra and changed trains were extremely complex and even signalmen controlling just home and distant signals were kept so busy identifying and logging as well as signalling that they would go many hours without food. Many were the confusions when mistakes were made. I recall standing with working timetable in hand at the ramp at the up end of the main down platform of St David's Exeter when the engine of a train signalled on the through platformless track halted opposite me. 'I'm number . . . and I thought I should stop here', shouted the driver. A hasty consultation of the timetable showed that he was right and we arranged that he would pull forward through the station and back into the down platform – points having to be locked by hand. I sprinted along the crowded platform to tell control who then had to organise an explanation over the public address system. An incident like that could of course hold up following trains for fifteen or twenty minutes. At the same point on another busy Saturday, a lengthy up *Atlantic Coast Express* failed to clear the points and a whole queue of following trains were delayed while the signalman found someone to tell the driver to pull up a few inches.

In theory, all Western Region main line trains carried their identification numbers on the front of the locomotive, and the signalmen at key points checked the train's identity and relayed information which was passed down the line, chalked up on notice boards and used on the public address systems. But engines failed and had to be replaced, the numbers got lost, the occasional crew just didn't care and one had the wonder of an unidentified train traversing the West like an interloping aircraft. There was often trouble, too, at Newton Abbot where (owing to lack of a turntable at Paignton) Torbay trains usually had their engines changed with one working tender first so as to be the right way round for an up train.

On peak days, as I have said, handling the crowds was like a military operation. Perhaps the most exciting time was on a Friday evening when normal routines were broken and up and down the system numerous shunting and stowing movements were made in readiness for the following morning. There was for instance a Friday train of restaurant cars from Paddington – cars and their crews to provide meals (to increase productivity ham salads only as the main course) on the packed Saturday trains. Incidentally, some of the crews spent the night in the refreshment department hostel which is now the publicity offices of David & Charles at Newton Abbot station. Trains would be stabled over Friday night at all kinds of unusual places – in the refuge siding at Teignmouth for the Teignmouth-Bradford service, on Southern metals at Exmouth for a Manchester service (unadvertised for many years because of that chronic lack of understanding between the regions serving the West that cost the taxpayer dearly and was a great disservice to the travelling public). At Churston was stabled a long train of ten-compartment pre-war GWR coaches, a Paddington-bound train that mopped up an exceptionally large number of passengers with its eighty seats per coach. And stock was worked down some of the branch lines (and again over Southern metals to Ilfracombe) for the summer Saturday specials to Paddington. The big stations were meanwhile piled high with luggage in advance – PLA, initials once understood instantly by everyone living in holiday areas. Everywhere there was an atmosphere of expectancy: it oozed out of the locomotive depots with their vast array of locomotives in readiness for the morrow.

The final goods trains ran very early on Saturday morning and by 3 am the down line was wholly devoted to passenger traffic. Overnight trains arrived from the North, Midlands and Paddington for both Cornwall, especially Newquay, and Torbay. Many made long, non-stop sprints, some technically not calling at Bristol or Plymouth, though in fact they did (maybe on the Bristol avoiding line and at Laira) for locomotive purposes. Signalboxes such as

Bishopsteignton and Kingskerswell opened early to shorten long sections. And by 5 am there could already be queues of trains following an early one running late – and residents of Kingskerswell would be wakened as engines, tender first, slipped on the dew-dampened rails trying to restart checked trains on the gradient on the Torbay line.

The overnight trains always had a reputation for running late, and on the busiest Saturdays when many ran in several parts the *average* late arrival at, say, Paignton could be as much as two hours. If it was as bad as this, then engines and stock were often not available to start return trips from Paignton to London, the Midlands or North in time, and so delays spread. At times, almost a half of the incoming holidaymakers arrived in their resorts by breakfast time. The railway's own refreshment rooms opened early. people living near stations like Torquay had no quiet especially on days with a large contingent of Welsh visitors who indulged in early morning song (and who sometimes sang again on the day before their departure to collect the fare home), and taxi services were flat out by 6 am. Of course these masses of incoming visitors could not go to their hotels or camps until noon or even later and were thus something of a liability to the resorts, swamping swimming pools and cafes (once a Paignton cafe sold 600 eggs at a Saturday breakfast time) and overfilling public shelters or just remaining on the station platforms when it was wet. Those who had not booked accommodation would form queues outside information bureaux before opening time.

Once the overnight trains had passed through there would be a slight lull on the down line, filled in by a few strictly local trains for the large numbers of Taunton and Exeter people going to the sea on day trips, until the first of the early morning departures from Paddington reached Exeter in mid morning. On the up line, however, once things started, there was no lull. Incoming visitors arrived partly overnight and partly by day by trains that may have had fairly similar starting times, the differing lengths of journeys meant staggered arrivals; but all returning visitors had the ambition to leave their resorts within the 7.30 am to 4.30 pm period and the great majority between 8.30 am and 12.30 pm. The return rush was always more concentrated, more vulnerable to things going wrong – and since every possible 'path' was utilised by advertised trains, extras could only be provided by extending the period of operation. And this was effectively only made possible by the introduction in various stages in the 1950s of compulsory booking. Individual seats were not bookable as on other days but all passengers travelling beyond Exeter from both Devonian and Cornish stations had to obtain a 'regulation' ticket and the number of tickets per train was limited to the number of seats expected to be available. When tickets for the popular mid-morning trains had been exhausted, people had to choose between an earlier or later start. Until this system was fully introduced it was common to see one train almost empty with another on the same route forty-five minutes later, at a more popular time, badly overcrowded.

As already stated, many overnight – and also some morning – trains were turned around at Paignton to provide 'up' services, and the same thing happened at Newquay and Penzance. When incoming trains were seriously late and 'up' departures were thus delayed, stations were besieged with crowds of waiting passengers. Under the regulation seat arrangements, passengers were not allowed on platforms until their train was nearly due, and when there was seriously late running several thousand people would be held in queues outside.

The majority of down trains stopped at Taunton, Exeter and Newton Abbot, with a fair number also at Dawlish and Teignmouth. More intensive use was made of the up line partly by making more trains run through non-stop over greater distances; for instance there was a thin mid-morning and midday service from Newton Abbot, Teignmouth and Dawlish to Exeter. At Exeter a calling express was usually overtaken by a 'flier' and the sight, sound and smell of a 'King' accelerating at full power, with home and distant signals down, through an otherwise choked station was one of the excitements of summer Saturday workings.

Another of the excitements was of course through trains to and from unusual destinations – in those days often fully equipped with roof-level destination boards such as 'Wolverhampton-Ilfracombe' and 'Paddington-Perranporth'. On the Western, summer Saturdays saw through workings to Minehead, Ilfracombe via Dulverton, Kingsbridge, Newquay, Falmouth, Perranporth and St Ives, as well as to Kingswear and Penzance. On the Southern, then not an inconsiderable rival for London traffic and once even with a through service via the Somerset & Dorset from the East Coast to Exmouth, the normal through coaches operated on services like the *Atlantic Coast Express* often became independent whole trains. There always seemed to be an *Atlantic Coast Express* at the central island platform at St David's.

By teatime on Saturdays the battle was largely over, whether it had been won, or lost with serious delays and red faces, and to the experienced eye stations and yards indeed looked like battlefields, with everything topsy turvy. Until extra sidings and other facilities were provided at Goodrington, near Paignton, in 1956, there was a chronic shortage of stabling for the day's later incoming trains – those not turned round to form upward services. The situation was worst on the last Saturday in July, the beginning of the peak fortnight, when many more visitors arrived than left and incoming expresses greatly exceeded leaving ones. Empty trains from Paignton had to be worked as far away as Bristol and even South Wales, and the string of empty stock extended the period of heavy occupation on the up line well into the evening – with for instance block to block working on the sea wall at Teignmouth and Dawlish. Even on the Barnstaple-Taunton line there were several empty stock trains working back from Ilfracombe, running at 40 mph through crossing stations thanks to the automatic token exchange fitted on that line and also the Minehead branch.

At the end of the season's peak fortnight, the reverse was of course the case. Empty trains had to be brought into the West from many parts of the country to uplift the returning crowds. Every inch of siding would be used by the Friday evening, and often parts of freight marshalling yards and goods loops and refuge sidings were commandeered also. In fact finding enough engines and rolling stock for the biggest return rush of the year was a problem that became progressively worse. Different districts vied with each other to hold back as much stock as possible, surreptitiously robbing mid-week excursions and ordinary trains of odd vehicles, keeping back the newer and better stock and quickly returning the shabbiest trains. And shabby indeed were the oldest trains: peeling paint of abandoned livery schemes on the outside, and frayed and dirty upholstery in the compartments. Much of the older stock was in poor condition even mechanically and often makeshift repairs had to be effected. The number of actual failures was remarkably

small, though when one did happen, such as a coach with a hot box
on an up express having to be shunted to the goods yard via the
down main line at the peak time one Saturday morning at
Starcross, literally dozens of following trains were disrupted.

To cope with the ever sharper peak demands, British Railways
maintained large fleets of vehicles used for only a few journeys a
year. Some were eventually used only twice yearly, at the beginning
and the end of the peak fortnight, beginning on the last Saturday
in July. This was the first Saturday that children at state schools
could go on holiday, and it was the start of a set holiday for much
Midland industry including most car factories. On top of that,
many people liked taking the peak fortnight since it included
August Bank Holiday and this gave a free Monday at home after
spending fourteen days by the sea. So great was the pressure that
some resorts did a third of their total season's trade during the
single fortnight. Because motor coach services could not increase their
capacity above that provided on other Saturdays, and a lower
proportion of industrial workers owned cars than did the profes-
sional and executive types who accounted for much of the early
and late season trade, the railways had to carry much more than
their fair share of the extra traffic. Many resort stations thus
received at least a third more passengers on the last Saturday in
July than on any other day of the year: to add to the pressure,
even many of the West Country's own factories closed down for
the peak fortnight, for instance hundreds instead of the usual
dozens of passengers booking at Wellington station between
Taunton and Exeter. Many branch lines had ten times their usual
number of passengers and collectively they absorbed a great
amount of extra rolling stock.

Retrospectively, it perhaps seems mad that the railways felt they
had an obligation not only to carry everyone but to try to do so
with the greatest possible comfort – or least possible discomfort.
It was a hopeless task, for as quickly as extra capacity was provided
so the numbers of peak fortnight visitors increased. In terms of
hotel and camp accommodation, too, the peak fortnight seemed to
be an unpluggable bottomless pit. Sadly, one has to tell that it was
the railways' extraordinary ability to carry such armies of people
that led to overcrowding in the resorts (many visitors wanting to
stay on the coast eventually found accommodation fifteen or more

miles inland) and a perpetuation of a highly unsatisfactory and wasteful state of affairs. I have already made the point that it took the impossible traffic jams caused by increasing car ownership to stagger both the season and the travelling week. But in the mid-1950s no railwayman struggling to provide every possible seat, every 'path', to put on duty every possible supernumerary porter, could have believed that in fact the whole act was anti-social — that the West Country's holiday trade and ultimately the railways themselves would have been better if less were done to accommodate the crowds.

In those days there was little analysis of the railways' various costs and receipts — just a bland assumption that there was a social duty to provide. Attitudes had indeed been hardly changed by the war or nationalisation — and however disreputable many cross-country holiday expresses may have been, the *Cornish Riviera Express* was hauled by a 'King' resplendent in the same green livery and the coaches were in the same chocolate and cream as pre-war. (The chocolate and cream livery was restored for a period for named trains only but the number of named trains increased and on summer Saturdays even the *Bristolian* set with its destination boards reversed worked into Devon.)

It was pretty obvious, though, that huge sums were being spent to carry the last few thousand people and to add slightly to the public's convenience by providing as many seats as possible. Not only had many of the trains used in the greatest rush of the year stood idle for the past 50 weeks but for every mile run in service during the peak there was often an empty mile as well. When things went well and such a train at least carried several hundred passengers on its revenue-earning run, there was at least some point in the exercise. But all too frequently it was these very extra-extra trains that got caught up in some muddle, leaving the depot late through a fault and losing their traffic to other services thus running heavily overcrowded, or somehow not being where they should be when they should be to carry the public. On the down line, for instance, there might be a delay of 45 minutes between any trains going west from Taunton; the first train after the gap would be terribly over-crowded having picked up at, say, Bristol people who should have used three or four trains and who, having waited a long time, could not know that other services with empty compartments would follow a few minutes later. Especially on journeys via Bristol to Devon and Cornwall a very large proportion of passengers joined or left at intermediate points often of course using connecting trains. So the costs incurred in providing that very last train could sometimes prove to be pointless.

It was when the Western Region later announced that no less than 14 per cent of its total income went on maintaining passenger stock that the ludicrousness of the situation became apparent. Inevitably there was then an over reaction, the new attitude being that trains could not pay unless they were used more or less continuously round the year. But of later developments, more anon.

The peak demands also strained the locomotive department to the hilt. Here however it was not so much the case of machines being kept serviceable just for peak demand (that would have been even more impossibly expensive) but of unsuitable machines being pressed into service. 2-8-0 tender goods locomotives on heavy passenger trains were one of the distinctive sights of summer Saturdays on the Western; in fact they were not all that unsuitable and often rendered yeoman service, but with their smaller wheels they could not match the speed of the 'Castles' and 'Kings'. 2-6-0 moguls were often used on sizeable mainline trains as well as being pushed hard on the Minehead and Barnstaple lines, while sometimes two smaller engines such as the 2-6-2 prairie tanks doubled up for one larger locomotive, especially on the Torbay and Newquay branches – though the Newquay branch was strengthened in the 1930s to accommodate 'Castles', some heavy trains required three engines (two front and one back) to take them up the bank.

Though most trains, such as the *Torbay Express,* were heavier than usual on Saturdays, it was not so much their own loads which necessitated longer running times as the slower pace inflicted by some of the Saturday-only services with less gallant motive power. In theory, such trains as the *Torbay Express* overtook their slower brethren at points like Taunton, Exeter and Newton Abbot but in practice – even when there was not total congestion and queueing – they were almost inevitably delayed west of Taunton by the slower movers.

The slower movers alas sometimes crawled. It could be a mere 20 mph up Wellington bank and a maximum of just under 60 on the downgrade through Cullompton. Trains halted at Kingskerswell could take 12 minutes to top the bank just before Torre. Two and a half hours was not uncommon with heavy trains between Taunton and Barnstaple, a period which could seem an eternity especially in a packed non-corridor coach. Virtually all trains were double headed over the gradients on the main line between Newton Abbot and Plymouth, but even so speeds were often very slow especially up Dainton bank where the clear bark of hardworking locomotives could be heard for the greater part of the day. In Cornwall too, there was considerable double heading of the longer trains but speeds were again often low. Many passengers bound for Newquay or Penzance who felt they had broken the back of the journey on reaching Taunton had in fact spent only 25-30 per cent of it timewise.

Yet despite my extensive personal experiences on Saturday after Saturday, year by year, I only recall two cases of trains failing completely with a broken down engine. Complete breakdowns were to follow by the score as diesels steadily took over from steam. The unreliability of the first diesels, the 'Warships', was vividly brought home when two trains collided outside Torquay station one Saturday evening. The first, halted by its failed diesel shortly after leaving the station, was run into by the steam locomotive of the second train which had also suffered a diesel failure earlier in the day. But, again, more of the later period anon.

Turning now to Saturday 27 July 1957, about which most of the rest of this book is specifically devoted, there were a number of special factors adding to traffic upon traffic. It was the beginning of the peak fortnight with masses of children just released from school and much Midland industry shut down. The total number of visitors was still growing more rapidly than car ownership, so that though the railway's proportion of business was declining its actual traffic increased until it reached an all time peak this day — helped by a national bus strike. Though some long-distance motor coaches ran as usual, people did not know what to expect and to make sure many extra long distance travellers came by train. Within the West there was enormous extra local travel, sometimes literally hundreds of day trippers, shoppers and so on joining trains with long-distance passengers already standing in the corridors.

In the Press, I wrote: 'British Railways bore the brunt . . . in any case it would have been the busiest day of the year — the one day on which traffic is so overwhelming that both overcrowding and long delays are inevitable. On Saturday, on top of all the usual day's traffic, especially from the Birmingham area, there were thousands of would be coach travellers to carry — and thousands of local passengers too. "No system on earth could be devised to carry such a volume of traffic smoothly," commented a spokesman at Exeter.

'Long distance expresses from Birmingham and the North arrived in South Devon considerably later than on any other summer day for many years. Nearly all were over an hour late, many over two hours, and some three hours.

'The greatest difficulty was experienced in clearing the line of empty trains at Paignton where many of the holiday expresses terminated. The result was that a queue of trains built up, one at each signal, until it stretched back to Dawlish Warren. Expresses due to run non-stop from Taunton to Newton Abbot were halted for up to 15 minutes on the sea wall at Teignmouth.

'Near Dawlish a man conducting a religious meeting included the passengers on a stopped train in his "congregation". At Kingskerswell, where there were more delays, passengers had a grand stand view of the carnival sports and joined in the applause.

'The railways' aim was to prevent overcrowding as far as possible even though it meant providing more trains than could be comfortably accommodated on the tracks. An unexpected source of trouble was a signalbox fire at Iver, on the Paddington main line, which delayed overnight trains to the West. As these were late arriving, there was a shortage of coaches, engines and staff to work return services.'

In other words it was not typical even of Saturdays at the beginning of the peak fortnight. Pressure was far greater than ever before not even excluding wartime evacuations from London. With the reduced signalling and other facilities now available, it would be totally impossible to move such traffic again. Every few minutes throughout the day crowded trains followed each other on their often snail's crawl west. Altogether over half a million passenger train journeys were made in Devon and Cornwall that day, well over 100,000 people travelling into the region from other parts of the country.

The table on page 30 shows the number of people arriving from Bristol or further away at some of the main stations in what was then the Exeter District of the Western Region:

AT	From Paddington and/or Waterloo	Bristol and beyond	North of England via Severn Tunnel	LMR Midland	South Wales	Stations via Didcot	North Warwick Line via Yate
Minehead	931	191	161	274	123	27	407
Taunton	492	554	105	158	296	47	88
Exeter (St David's)	470	305	372	662	405	175	257
Dawlish	768	161	125	343	176	33	186
Teignmouth	923	174	321	255	132	77	623
Newton Abbot	171	77	77	69	65	26	46
Torre	352	159	303	188	213	35	15
Torquay	4769	1324	3261	2771	1091	592	2625
Paignton	3009	1649	1273	2261	1029	428	2980
Ilfracombe	1894	527	1350	826	373	175	325

Some of these figures may seem small to the uninitiated or to those bewitched by the claims of patronage put out by individual resorts — claims that if added together would sometimes show that one and a half times the entire British population was on holiday simultaneously. These are of course figures based on the number of actual tickets collected. Such was the pressure that after arriving up to three hours late many people had to queue 15 minutes to pass through the ticket barrier and then an hour for a taxi at places like Torquay. Incidentally, taking into account traffic to stations not listed in the table, about 32,000 passengers making journeys of at least 100 miles travelled down the Torbay line alone, while local traffic included 3,000 people going just from Torquay to Paignton. The pressure on ancillary services such as telephones and cloak-rooms (4,000 items of luggage were left at Torquay station's cloakroom) was correspondingly great. It proved quite impossible to advise people waiting at stations how late particular trains were running, and with even show pieces like the *Torbay Express* two hours late, car parks were more congested than ever before or since. An AA official who drove me to St David's at Exeter said, 'I thought we had been dealing with a rush on the roads but this is nothing to what they've got here.'

Perhaps the best way to fill in some of the background to the summer Saturday working is to comment on what happened at some of the more important points on the system.

Taunton. Taunton station was a schoolboy's dream on the busiest Saturdays with roughly speaking alternate main line expresses stopping and passing through at speed, whistles shrilly sounding, with a few expresses to and from Minehead and Ilfracombe being divided on the down line and joined on the up, and with lots of local trains all themselves far busier than usual — locals to Exeter (though their number and also the stops they made was greatly reduced to keep the line free for expresses), Barnstaple, Ilfracombe, Castle Cary, Yeovil and Chard. Expresses from Paddington and Bristol normally sustained high speed through Somerset right into Taunton station, the flyover junction at Cogload where the two routes join being one of the best pieces of GWR pre-war investment. 'We came quickly to Taunton and got stuck' was the familiar cry of holiday travellers, for onward to Exeter there was only a single pair of tracks to carry the traffic.

If trains from the Paddington and Bristol routes were ready to leave Taunton simultaneously, one would inevitably be delayed six or seven minutes behind the other on Wellington bank. True, the quadrupled track stretched through Taunton to Norton Fitzwarren two miles ahead, but this did not help the Wellington bank bottleneck and anyway Norton Fitzwarren was under considerable strain getting the down Minehead, Barnstaple and Ilfracombe trains from the down relief over the down and up mains to their respective branches. On the busiest Saturdays the number of trains going down the two branches totalled over 30.

Taunton-Exeter. As already stated, the bottleneck was Wellington bank, up from Wellington station to Whiteball tunnel on the border of Somerset and Devon. It remained a bottleneck even though an intermediate block signal was provided since many trains topped the bank at less than 20 mph − and if a stop were made for a banking engine at Wellington that in itself would waste valuable line occupancy. In fact one of the problems was the uncertainty of the supply of banking engines. At least twice, I was on heavy trains whose engine drivers whistled and slowed on approaching Wellington only to be waved on by the signalman since no banker was available − and without a running start that indeed meant a slogging crawl up the last half mile. However, if there had not been a bottleneck on Wellington bank one would have developed elsewhere. The trains had to be 'spaced out in the country', and normally once they were clear of the bank there was a fair chance of a smooth ride down through Cullompton to Exeter − providing the driver of say a 'Castle' bore in mind that the train immediately ahead probably had a less sprintful steed than his own.

Exeter. Here perhaps I may quote an article that appeared in *The Western Morning News* on 17 August 1953 when summer Saturday traffic was still increasing rapidly − an article which, I cannot resist adding, was later several times borrowed by railwaymen asked to give lectures on their own job.

ON HOLIDAY IN THE WEST
MORE THAN A MERE RAILWAY STATION
West's most important junction
EXETER ST DAVID'S is more than a mere railway station. For over a century it has been one of the most important institutions in the Westcountry, and on its platforms have been enacted

many historic scenes.

The station – though the old roof has gone and the gauge of the rails is now different – is still essentially the same as when the first train arrived from London by way of Bristol on Brunel's newly-opened Bristol and Exeter Railway.

Throughout its career St David's has been the most important station in the West. Through it one recent Saturday passed an estimated 120,000 passengers. On a normal summer Saturday, between 9 am and 4 pm, no fewer than 130 long-distance expresses either stop or pass through the station.

St David's is important as a stopping place on the main Western Region Line from Paddington to Penzance, and here some Plymouth-bound expresses shed their tails for the Torquay line.

All the year round the city provides St David's with heavy traffic, while the Teign Valley and Exe Valley branch trains pop in and out as best they can between the expresses. There are in addition, on the main line, local trains to Taunton and stopping trains to Newton Abbot and Paignton.

London connection

What really makes the station important as a junction is the connection with the Southern Region line from Waterloo to the West. Through the station pass all Southern trains on the lines to Ilfracombe, Bideford and Torrington, Bude, Padstow, and Plymouth Friary.

There is a constant interchange of passengers between Western and Southern trains, while the trains of the two Regions are forever cutting across each others' routes.

When an express from Waterloo runs down from Exeter Central Station into St David's it crosses and prevents movement on the main Paddington-Penzance line. Similarly, when a Southern train from Ilfracombe or Bude arrives at Cowley Bridge Junction (just over a mile to the north of St David's) it blocks both main lines of the old Great Western.

In St David's Station, Southern trains usually keep to themselves in the two middle platforms, numbers three and four, Western trains using platforms one and two for down trains and the Exe Valley 'locals', and five and six for up trains.

Plan shelved

It is at the approaches to the station, where both Regions share the same lines, that delays are bound to occur when traffic is dense.

Pre-war there was a plan to make St David's a two-storey station, Southern Railway trains being kept quite independent on lines and platforms built above the existing layout. Such a station would reduce delays to traffic, but its cost would be very great, and it is hardly likely to be built while Plymouth Northroad is still in its present state.

On Saturday I spent a long time examining the way in which the heavy week-end holiday traffic was being handled. Though crowds were not so great as over the immediate Bank Holiday period, many thousands of holidaymakers were on the move.

Most trains were no more than comfortably full, but there were a few unfortunate exceptions. It is always difficult to estimate the number of passengers who will be using each train, and in several instances more turned up than had been expected.

Often, however, when people were crowded in the corridor in the middle coaches, there were spare seats at the front or back of the train. Holidaymakers too readily assume there are no seats and even when told there is room they are reluctant to move along the corridor.

At St David's on Saturday the chief cause of delay was the constant criss-cross movement of Western and Southern trains. At one time there were five trains standing at the platforms, all ready to leave at the same time. Obviously only one could move off in each direction at the identical moment, and the other three (already late) were delayed further.

If everything went exactly according to the timetable, there would never be more than one waiting to go in each direction.

The timetable graph for the up track between Exeter and Taunton is drawn on the assumption that there must be an interval of seven minutes between the passing of each train through Whiteball tunnel, which divides Devon from Somerset.

Movement problem

If trains for Taunton could leave St David's at intervals of seven minutes, and if they all ran at the same speed, there would never be delays. To keep the trains moving at the same speed and with the same space intervals between them is the aim of the Operating Department. But theory is one thing and practice another.

Coming from Newton Abbot some trains stop at Teignmouth and Dawlish, while others do not. If a train from Cornwall is late, one from Paignton may be allowed to run in front of it.

But if the Paignton one stops at Teignmouth and Dawlish and the Cornish one does not, both trains may arrive at Exeter within two minutes of each other. Then it is quite possible that both will be ready to leave at the same time. Meanwhile, a Southern train for Ilfracombe might also be waiting to leave.

Some Western expresses stop at St David's and some do not, some that do stop take longer to load passengers than others, while some trains are delayed by the activities of the Southern route, and others have a clear run. The theoretical seven-minute interval disappears.

Thus on Saturday, after there had been an interval of 20 minutes during which no train for the Taunton route had left, within six minutes three expresses started following each other in procession.

Because for safety reasons nearly seven minutes must elapse between the passing of each through Whiteball tunnel, the second train would have taken five minutes longer than the first to reach Taunton, and the third five minutes longer again than the second.

Because best use can be made of the track if all trains run at about the same speed, the crack expresses, such as the *Cornish Riviera,* are slower on Saturdays than other days, while many local trains are cancelled, and other trains stop at fewer stations.

A local train stopping at each station between Exeter and Taunton takes as much time on the track as three expresses. And the expresses must be got through. Here is reconstructed the story of what happened during one hour at St David's on August 8.

One hour's traffic

The movements described are only those of passenger trains. Shunting operations and the movement of banking engines – those that whistle violently before they assist a train up the steep incline to Central Station – are not mentioned.

During the chosen hour, 12.10 pm to 1.10 pm, no fewer than 26 passenger trains come into the picture. I have numbered them 1 to 26. The time following the number of train is the time at which it started, passed through, or arrived at the station.

Following the time there appears either the letter (D) or (U), standing for down and up. In order to follow the sequence of movements it must be remembered that a Southern and a Western train for London leave St David's in opposite directions.

But for convenience I have marked all trains with the letter (D) or (U) according to whether they were on the down or up main Western line.

15,000 passengers

The time shown in parenthesis is that at which the train was scheduled to leave its starting place.

(1) 12.5 (D) Plymouth Friary (9.50) to Portsmouth, arrived.

(2) 12.8 (U) Exeter Central (11.49) to Plymouth Friary, arrived.

(3) 12.8 (D) Walsall (6.35) to Kingswear, arrived.

(4) 12.10 (U) Paignton (10.35) to Wolverhampton, passed overtaking train number 2.

(1) 12.10 (D) Plymouth Friary (9.50) to Portsmouth, left.

(2) 12.13 (U) Exeter Central (11.49) to Plymouth Friary, left.

(5) 12.17 (U) Paignton (10.10) to Cardiff, arrived.

(6) 12.17 (D) Paddington (8.25) to Penzance, passed overtaking train number 3.

(3) 12.18 (D) Walsall (6.35) to Kingswear, left.

(7) 12.19 (U) First part of Paignton (11.00) to Nottingham (ie the first part started at Exeter), left.

(8) 12.20 (D) Ilfracombe (10.30) to Waterloo, arrived.

(5) 12.23 (U) Paignton (10.10) to Cardiff, left.

(8) 12.25 (D) Ilfracombe (10.30) to Waterloo, left.

(9) 12.25 (D) Paddington (8.50) to Paignton, arrived.

(10) 12.28 (U) Kingswear (10.20) to Crewe, passed.

(11) 12.32 (U) Newquay (8.10) to Newcastle, passed.

(9) 12.34 (D) Paddington (8.50) to Paignton, left.

(12) 12.35 (U) Second part of Paignton (11.00) to Nottingham, arrived.

(13) 12.39 (D) Wolverhampton (6.55) to Paignton, arrived.

(14) 12.39 (U) Torquay (11.30) to Paddington, arrived.

(15) 12.39 (U) Waterloo (8.22) to Ilfracombe, arrived.

(Note: Three trains arrived simultaneously, and there were now three all waiting to use the rails to Cowley Bridge, a fourth train waiting at the same time on the down platform.)

(12) 12.40 (U) Second part of Paignton (11.00) to Nottingham, left.

(15) 12.43 (U) Waterloo (8.22) to Ilfracombe, left.

(16) 12.44 (D) Torrington (10.48) to Waterloo, arrived

(13) 12.45 (D) Wolverhampton (6.55) to Paignton, left.

(14) 12.46 (U) Torquay (11.30) to Paddington, left.

(17) 12.48 (D) Paddington (7.30) to Kingswear, arrived.

(16) 12.49 (D) Torrington (10.48) to Waterloo, left

(18) 12.52 (D) Paddington (9.30) to Newquay, passed overtaking train number 17.

(19) 12.52 (U) Penzance (7.30) to Wolverhampton, passed.

(17) 12.55 (D) Paddington (7.30) to Kingswear, left.

(20) 12.55 (D) Plymouth Friary (11.00) to Brighton, arrived.

(21) 12.58 (U) Perranporth (8.15) to Paddington, passed.

(20) 1.00 (D) Plymouth Friary (11.00) to Brighton, left.

(22) 1.2 (U) Falmouth (8.35) to Paddington, passed.

(23) 1.2 (U) Waterloo (8.35) to Ilfracombe, arrived.

(24) 1.3 (D) Leicester (6.40) to Paignton, arrived.

(25) 1.7 (U) Exeter (12.45) to Taunton, local train, left.

(26) 1.8 (D) Paddington (9.40) to Paignton, passed overtaking train 24.

(23) 1.10 (U) Waterloo (8.35) to Ilfracombe, left.

(24) 1.13 (D) Leicester (6.40) to Paignton, left.

That is what happens during a typical hour. During that time well over 15,000 passengers would have passed through the station.

30,000 travellers

Forty-five per cent of them would be looking forward to a holiday, forty-five per cent regretting their holiday was finished, and ten per cent going about their ordinary business and feeling sorry for themselves that they had to travel on such a day.

Details in the accompanying table [page 38] show how in a few hours on July 25 over 30,000 long-distance passengers arrived at eight of the principal stations in the Exeter District of the Western

	A	B	C	D	E	F	G	Total
Taunton	290	267	122	119	242	47	32	1119
Minehead	889	302	163	319	86	66	236	2061
Exeter	450	215	350	398	350	185	171	2119
Dawlish	311	150	113	290	68	28	186	1146
Teignmouth	624	171	107	240	101	458	413	2114
Newton Abbot	294	266	135	203	87	17	23	1045
Torquay	4261	876	1441	2031	919	279	1735	11542
Paignton	2095	1394	1013	1789	740	118	1886	9035

Region. Can you wonder that things do not always go smoothly?

A stands for passengers from Paddington, B for those from the Bristol area, C from the North, D from the London Midland line, E from South Wales, F stations via Didcot, and G the North Warwick line to Birmingham and Wolverhampton.

The more we are together the happier we shall be? Well, nobody would choose to travel in trains slower and more crowded than on ordinary days. But with all the inconvenience necessary while the present holiday system persists, the holiday atmosphere still wins.

Exeter was of course the focal point, the crossroads of the West's rail system, though in those days the two regions scarcely took more notice of each other than in GWR and LSWR days. Large numbers of people did however change from one to the other while many Western Region passengers alighted from expresses making their next stop at Plymouth to join those calling at Dawlish, Teignmouth and Newton Abbot. The main down platform was indeed often the most crowded – and when several hundred passengers alighted in the bay platform at Exeter St David's off the Exe Valley train at the beginning of Heathcoat's holiday fortnight at Tiverton they might have almost to fight their way off. Four ticket collectors were on duty at the gates – and Teign Valley passengers had to pass through the gates to join a bus to Alphington since at the peak of the rush the valley's autocar was not allowed on the main line rails. I often wish someone had made a film with sound of those days, with two tank engines backing on to yet another train labelled the *Atlantic Coast Express* to help it up to Central, drivers of 'fliers' peering out of their cabs to see if signals were changing in their favour, the harassed level crossing keeper at the up end of the station asking road users to be patient, an Exe Valley train cheekily emerging from the bay and crossing to the up main, and six trains often being in view at once from the up end of the down platform including almost inevitably a down one held at Riverside signalbox's starting signal waiting entry into the station or even just clearance of the through road pending a Southern or other movement.

Exeter-Newton Abbot. Frequently trains worked block-to-block, stopping or being at least slowed at every signalbox. The main problem was the mixture of non-stop trains and those calling at Dawlish and Teignmouth — other intermediate stations having virtually no service during peak hours. A train of 15 coaches disgorging 100 passengers each at Dawlish and Teignmouth would delay a non-stop express by anything up to 15 minutes. An express not stopping at Exeter could sometimes overtake there to give a sensible priority West, but as most trains stopped at Exeter and there was only a single down platform for Western use, frequently a train calling at Dawlish and so on left immediately in front of one that did not. Loop lines were available at Exminster and Dawlish Warren where trains were sometimes halted to be overtaken by the non-stop Newton Abbot or Plymouth services. But whatever efforts were made to avoid it, on the busiest days inevitably queueing developed on the sea wall. From one train you could often see that in front and behind as well as three travelling — or waiting to travel — in the opposite direction. When conditions were at their worst, it made no difference anyway since the queueing was not a local matter of trains stopping at Dawlish and Teignmouth but of congestion in Newton Abbot and indeed possibly as far ahead as Paignton. For when Paignton could not dispose quickly enough of a succession of trains arriving there, following services could occupy every possible position back to Dawlish Warren or Starcross.

Newton Abbot. Locomotive work made Newton a crucial point. Virtually all Plymouth and Cornwall trains, whether advertised to call or not, stopped to pick up a second engine, while most Torbay line trains at least in the earlier part of the day changed engines, the new one being that which worked the return train or empty stock back from Paignton or Kingswear. Most engine crews were changed, too, duties being allocated from a hut at the down end of the down platform around which up to 40 or 50 enginemen would be clustered waiting their turn. When all trains were late, men had to wait an hour or occasionally even three hours before actually starting work. Newton had three passenger tracks each for up and down traffic, two of them with platforms. Frequently all three down tracks were in use simul-taneously, a new train running in just as soon as one moved out, though obviously only non-stopping trains could be routed by the non-platform road. This of course was the point at which Plymouth and Cornwall trains held back by queueing caused by trouble at

Paignton were set free, hopefully for a clear run up Dainton bank. On the up side, too, it often happened that all three tracks were occupied — by trains wanting to depart simultaneously — and of course going east all had to use the single up track to Exeter and Taunton. But with the three tracks in the station as well as facilities for holding trains outside, and switching from the (Plymouth) relief to the (Torbay) main or vice versa at Aller Junction, at least Newton could despatch up trains in a sensible order.

Newton Abbot-Paignton. These few miles frequently took more than an hour! There were all kinds of problems. Paignton, the terminus for three-quarters of the Torbay line holiday expresses, had only a single platform for traffic in each direction tightly sandwiched between busy level crossings. In fact there was a scissors crossover to enable trains to arrive or depart from either platform but when traffic was heavy in both directions there was little to be gained from using it. Siding accommodation in Paignton itself was very limited, and even when new sidings and a turntable were belatedly opened at Goodrington, a mile further on at the end of the double track, disposing of empty trains took too long. As if that were not bad enough, such was the up line gradient between Torquay and Torre that whatever the locomotive there had to be a banker for trains over 10 bogies. Attaching and detaching bankers and finding paths for returning light engines from Torre to Torquay lost a great deal more time — in fact so much that after the disastrous performance on 27 July 1957 it was decided to limit almost all up trains off the Torbay line to the load of a single locomotive, nine or ten coaches. Only by doing this was it possible to get down trains on to the Torbay line quickly enough to prevent the queue stretching back to the main line snarling up Plymouth and Cornish traffic. Even then it was common not only just on the busiest Saturday of the year but ten or a dozen Saturdays for Paignton-bound trains to be unable to leave the platform at Newton Abbot when they were ready to do so, and then to be halted at Aller Junction, Kingskerswell, Torre, Torquay, Gas House Siding, and outside Paignton. Of these the shortest delay by signal would most probably be at Torquay simply because getting people off took longer there before the train was ready to leave. The provision of even one extra platform at Torquay would have been a blessing. London trains shown as starting there had to be worked empty up

from Paignton except that one was worked down empty from
Torre where it had been stabled overnight and another sometimes
from Newton Abbot.

Paignton-Kingswear. About a third of the expresses continued
to Kingswear, over the steeply graded single track with a crossing
loop at Churston, junction for Brixham, and considerable ingenuity
had to be used to prevent 'fouling up' this section. In fact the
number of Saturday workings did not — and could not — greatly
exceed the peak summer Monday-to-Friday ones, but trains were
longer and came and went to more different destinations. Total
priority was naturally given to up services — providing the stock
and engines had arrived at Kingswear. As mentioned earlier, one
up Paddington express composed of ten-compartment coaches used
to make an early morning start at Churston which thus — like
Teignmouth — contributed its small mite to the Friday night
storage problem.

Newton Abbot-Plymouth. The two inclines each way, of which
the chief was Dainton on the down line rising sharply immediately
after Aller Junction, and the longer but not quite so steep
Hemerdon rising immediately after Plympton on the up line,
obviously set the tone of Newton Abbot-Plymouth working. With
the other major gradients rising on either side of Totnes, it was
simpler to provide bankers (or strictly speaking assisting engines
in the front) throughout between Newton and Plymouth than to
stop and start for attaching and detaching and get involved in light
engine working. Though traffic beyond Newton Abbot was much
lighter than on the Taunton-Newton stretch, sections at least in
terms of time taken on the upgrade in them were much longer,
meaning that queueing could develop as elsewhere. In fact it was
usually the time taken to climb Dainton and Hemerdon that determined the distance between trains, and in both cases there was such
complete occupation that often trains were halted at the foot
waiting their turn and thus lacked a running start.

The CWR's rule was that locomotive power should be great enough
to restart trains if stopped anywhere but the four inclines were
exceptions — and to give a modicum of initial help waiting trains
in fact stopped just short of the beginning of the gradient. This
meant that even if they were signalled over the intersections of
the Torbay line, Plymouth-bound drivers of checked trains

preferred to stop short of Aller Junction box. Though most trains were double headed and therefore lacked spectacular interest from the point of locomotive performance, very hard working was often involved and when standing on the top of Dainton tunnel (an increasingly popular venue for enthusiasts at the end of the steam era) you could often tell how skilful each of the drivers was being.

Like other non-resort main-line stations, those between Newton and Plymouth lost many of their Saturday trains in an effort to keep long-distance wheels moving, and such strictly local trains as did call at places like Cornwood were not started until all the expresses which should precede them had gone — leaving small groups of passengers only wanting to travel a few miles and not understanding the reason for the delay determined to go by bus, or even cycle, next time. Brent had a few more trains including that setting down and picking up the summer Saturday-only through Paddington-Kingsbridge coaches, and Totnes a few more again, trains starting the climbs on either side from scratch usually delaying following non-stop ones.

Plymouth. After years of doubt and delay Plymouth North Road's rebuilding begun in the 1930s was only completed in time for the opening ceremony to be conducted by the man who would quickly render some of its accommodation superfluous — Dr Beeching. Throughout the 1950s, there were only two platforms available for down trains plus the Southern's up services from Friary via Tavistock to Exeter. The platforms could only be approached slowly, and many trains shed restaurant car and other coaches as well as changing engines. So it was a slow business, frequently preceded by a wait outside Mutley tunnel, which in turn blocked one of the busiest sections of double track in Britain, carrying not only the Western main line services but engines to and from Laira shed, the Tavistock and Launceston services, the Southern trains to and from Friary, and even auto cars to and from their separate depot at Laira. Even on Mondays to Fridays, trains and engines worked block to block much of the day, Mannamead signalbox between North Road East and Laira having a high grading though no points. An intermediate block signal would have served equally well since no points were provided. On normal days, however, efforts were made to keep the line free for principal expresses; no such concession was possible on summer Saturdays when such was the pressure on the station that it was occasionally easier to switch coaches from the up side to the down side by working them on a local train to Tavistock and back, than to shunt them in situ. Incidentally, for some years there was a Tavistock North to Tavistock South lunch time through train provided to cut shunting movement in Plymouth. Some pressure was also taken off the station by changing locomotives of non-stopping expresses at Laira, though this had to be done on the main line. (The down *Cornish Riviera* changed engines at Newton Abbot and then ran non-stop to Truro.) Pre-war plans included quadrupling Mutley tunnel and a short section of quadrupled track was laid at Laira, but this part of the scheme was dropped.

Cornwall. This book is mainly concerned with Devon plus the main line from Taunton but a few notes on Cornish practice may add to the picture. The first hazard was the single-track Royal Albert Bridge over the Tamar with 15 mph restriction, of course particularly time-consuming in the passage of 15 coach trains with two engines. But almost all the 80 miles from Plymouth to Penzance had a hazard of one kind or another and on the busiest days every signalman would have to halt up or down trains because the section ahead had not cleared. The worst bank was that on the up line from Lostwithiel through Bodmin Road. The number of up trains stopping at Bodmin Road was kept to a minimum and any that called might delay the next three non-stopping services.

Pressure on the main line of course eased after Par with the loss of the Newquay trains, but Truro indulged in its own scenes of peak chaos and even after the loss of through services to Falmouth, Perranporth and St Ives (in fact only one each and St Ives only part of the *Cornish Riviera*) there was often section-to-section working through to Penzance and at times heavy pressure on its distinctive terminal with its ugly wooden roof. All Cornish branches were busier on Saturdays though those to Looe, Bodmin and Wadebridge, Fowey and Helston kept themselves isolated from the operating point of view.

The Newquay line on the other hand was very much part of the wider system with through trains (sometimes run in two parts) to and from Midland and Northern cities as well as Paddington. As has already been mentioned, three engines were sometimes used on the twisting and turning gradients, especially up Luxulyan bank in the down direction. Because of the long sections of single track and the inadequacy of some of the crossing loops (St Columb for instance could not cross two full-length trains) services were run in batteries. First in the day came a succession of overnight expresses disgorging crowds at Newquay before breakfast; then the emphasis turned to up services with morning departures including for some years an express advertised as non-stop Paddington; and in afternoon and early evening the daytime expresses poured in. Enthusiasts making their first trip down the Newquay line were apt to be surprised first by the extreme ruggedness, gradients and curvature of much of the route and secondly by the vastness of Newquay's station with its three long platforms, two capable of taking double-headed trains of 15 bogies, its array of sidings, rolling stock and locomotives. Up to 7,000 passengers travelling from at least as far away as Bristol arrived here on peak Saturdays.

The Southern. The Southern's story only indirectly concerns us here, but in its heyday the Waterloo-Exeter line, its continuation in North Devon and Cornwall as 'the withered arm', and its East Devon branches carried a considerable volume of holiday traffic as indeed did also the cross-country Somerset & Dorset making connections with the Waterloo-Exeter route at Templecombe. The main feature of the Southern was the large number of places served by through services from London – Lyme Regis, Seaton, Sidmouth, Exmouth, Ilfracombe, Torrington, Bude, Padstow and Plymouth. Some places normally having a single through coach sported a whole train or major part of one on Saturdays, a number of restaurant cars working through beyond Exeter to Ilfracombe and Okehampton. This reduced the amount of joining and dividing of trains at Exeter Central, platform occupancy there governing the line's total volume – though sometimes the governing factor was the time taken by down trains to climb Honiton bank and a queue would form back from Axminster.

Timekeeping on the Southern was however usually good, at least to Exeter, punctual Waterloo trains often crossing over Manchester-Bournemouth ones hours late on the Somerset & Dorset. A Cleethorpes-Birmingham-Exmouth service introduced via the Somerset & Dorset was of course not so reliable. At Exeter St David's the Southern sometimes demonstrated its superiority by bringing in a Waterloo train on time opposite a Paddington train that had left

London an hour or more earlier. But travelling by the Southern beyond Exeter was a dreary business. First, a long wait at Central where even if there was not actual dividing of the train into sections serving different places, some coaches usually came off and the 'Merchant Navy' class locomotives were replaced by the 'West Country' class, then an equally long wait at St David's, the Western exercising its rights inherited from the GWR to treat Waterloo trains in a paltry way albeit on the busiest days there was a genuine problem to fit the Southern's services in.

The greater number of Southern passengers were bound for Ilfracombe. One of the few agreements reached between the rival systems serving the West in pre-war days was that both would stop spending on improving their routes to North Devon. The agreement was made after the GWR had installed automatic token exchanges on its Taunton-Barnstaple line and even opened a triangular junction to prevent summer Ilfracombe-bound trains having to call and reverse at its own Barnstaple terminus. The Southern however had neither completed the doubling of the track from Coleford Junction (where the North Devon route left the Plymouth one) nor lengthened crossing loops to accommodate full-length trains. Crossing two holiday expresses at places like Eggesford therefore meant setting one of them back over hand-locked points into the refuge siding — an undignified not to mention time-consuming operation. The Southern's route to Barnstaple was therefore slow and erratic though with its level track bed and bridges prepared for doubling it could so easily have been made good; the Western's from Taunton was appallingly graded but with automatic token exchanges and crossing loops laid for 40 mph running could in practice be reasonable, though the triangular junction was not reopened after the war.

Between them the two routes fed a prodigious number of trains to be handled at a cramped Barnstaple Junction, a single-platform Barnstaple Town and a mighty steep bank up to Mortehoe and Woolacombe. Almost every heavy Saturday express had to be banked up to the summit in both directions, the gradient in the up direction starting so immediately at Ilfracombe station that shunting engines sometimes had to make several attempts before they could clear points to switch stock from one track to another. Up to 10,000 people arrived by train at stations on the Ilfracombe line on summer Saturdays, enginemen not infrequently feeling heroes in getting there with heavy loads against uneven odds — including the sheer perverse geography — while passengers calculated how much quicker they could have reached East or South Devon resorts or gone by car, though the breathtaking views of the sea from Mortehoe & Woolacombe and again just before Ilfracombe clifftop terminus brought them relief.

Bude and Padstow trains left the main Plymouth line at Okehampton, a busy station at times, and finally went their separate ways over the impoverished North Cornwall — North Devon plateau land at Halwill Junction which also had its moments of intense activity; but the Saturday density of trains here was not so greatly different from the Monday-to-Friday one. The trains were just heavier, and some superb locomotive work was done especially by the elderly 'Greyhounds', the 4-4-0 T9s, on the Padstow line, laid out and maintained as a main line and capable of sustained 60-70 mph running over many downhill sections.

CHAPTER III

The Contrast with Today

Each year since 1957 has seen a reduction both in the number of trains run on peak Saturdays and in the facilities provided for them. Yet it is only fair to stress at the beginning of an assessment of more recent developments that the basic all-the-year-round Monday-to-Friday service on the Western Region main line into Devon and Cornwall is far superior: trains are both quicker and more numerous than anyone imagined possible in steam days. In winter mid-week the GWR seldom ran more than six trains from Paddington to the South West via the direct Castle Cary line. Today there is a train throughout the year every hour of the day from 7.30 am till 7.30 pm, many of them travelling quicker than the single best service in steam days. Two extra trains run down from Paddington on Friday evenings and the return service on Sunday evenings has been totally revolutionised. All these improvements have been achieved surprisingly cheaply since rolling stock and locomotive power are utilised as never before.

And it is of course this emphasis on getting the most out of equipment that has enabled the railways to see so much of their peak Saturday traffic disappear without worry Before the war, and even in the years immediately after it, trains were run to carry the traffic presenting itself as a social responsibility. Nobody enquired into the cost. When cost analysis began and particularly when it was discovered that 14 per cent of all the Western Region's income went on upkeeping existing passenger rolling stock, rationalisation was inevitable. To begin with the railway management almost gratefully saw the peak demand decline, enabling scrapping of rolling stock and of some track and signalling facilities which had been expensively maintained maybe for only half a dozen days' full use a year. Reducing the number of trains by a quarter made a much greater proportionate saving. Conversely, having almost welcomed the beginning of the decline in the peak traffic, the railways were certainly slow to realise that without a forcible sales drive the time would come when many empty seats would be left even on trains that could be comfortably run out of ordinary resources. Today the loss of traffic on a summer Saturday is already a real loss; and ultimately one feels that there might be no more trains on a summer Saturday than in winter mid-week. Given the lull in freight movement, that would be a real waste of capacity.

The decline has been helped by the dramatic reduction in the number of places served by through trains. From the 1972 summer the Beeching Plan is fulfilled in one respect: no trains reach the Atlantic cum Bristol Channel coast between Newquay and Weston-super-Mare. And no resort on the Dorset-Devon coast is on the railway system between Weymouth and Exmouth. Against that, the average speed, reliability and comfort of the main-line services is far higher than even a few years ago. The journey from London to Torbay by comfortable restaurant car train can often be done on a summer Saturday in less than half the time it takes by road, not allowing for a stop for a meal. Yet few people are wealthy enough or prepared to travel light enough to leave their own car at home, take the train for speed and hire a car for touring at the other end. The car-hire business remains miniscule in the South West. Only with the special motor-rail services does the railway really cater for the summer car-owning holidaymaker – though quite a few people taking short secondary holidays do so by train. And though the motor-rail trains add something to revenue, the numbers of cars and people they carry are small, and as with the old peak season expresses, the rolling stock is only utilised a fraction of the year.

There has of course been a vast reduction in the amount of physical railway. Taunton's middle island platform is no longer used by passengers, and the track is no longer quadrupled from Taunton to Norton Fitzwarren. Exminster has been shorn of many of its sidings and rarely does empty passenger stock now have to be stored that far away from Torbay. Intermediate signalboxes that used to open to help with the peak rush at places like Powderham and Parson's Tunnel have been closed and demolished, while Dawlish's signalbox which used to be open continuously now only comes to life on peak Saturdays. No signalbox remains between Teignmouth and Newton Abbot East. Plymouth has been shorn of all its Millbay branch network including the former passenger sidings (though the modernised Plymouth station is far more convenient than that available when traffic was at its peak); and Truro is among other places where many sidings have disappeared.

The branches from Taunton to Minehead and Barnstaple (for Ilfracombe), from Brent to Kingsbridge, and Chacewater to Perranporth have all not merely lost their through services but been totally closed. Falmouth and St Ives also no longer have through trains, the layout at their terminal stations now being a single track ending at a buffer stop. Only two branches continue to be served by expresses: the Torbay line and the Newquay branch. Paignton can still be something of a bottleneck on the busiest Saturdays, and until 1971 some use was still made of the sidings provided at Goodrington under British Railways' first modernisation plan (though the locomotive turntable did not last long after dieselisation). On other days the Paignton-Kingswear section is run as a self-contained branch, but until 1971 the successor to the *Torbay Express* (the name is no longer used) continued to Kingswear on summer Saturdays. Facilities have been greatly reduced over the Newquay branch but a handful of through services still reach this most successful Cornish resort, including one or two of the remaining overnight Friday/Saturday services from up-country to the West. The decline of the use of these services has been particularly sharp as more people dislike the discomfort of night trains without sleeping cars and as the following morning's daylight services have become speedier and more reliable.

Very much less remains of the former Southern's traffic, and through services like that from Cleethorpes via Birmingham and the Somerset & Dorset to Sidmouth and Exmouth now seem so distant as to belong to a totally different age. The Southern effectively terminates at Exeter these days and at most one extra service is normally run that far on summer Saturdays. The former continuation between Exeter and Barnstaple carried one through train to and from Paddington on peak 1971 Saturdays, but otherwise all that is now left of the 'withered arm' is the suburban

Plymouth-Bere Alston-Gunnislake section. Ilfracombe, Bideford, Bude and Wadebridge are all far removed from trains, yet only eight years ago railwaymen working on the Ilfracombe line were genuinely and sincerely shocked at the suggestion that the track should be singled, believing that it would be impossible to handle the traffic still then presenting itself at the height of the season. Exmouth had its railway reprieved from the Beeching Plan but the lack of bustle is now as noticeable there as at Exeter Central, scene of never-ending activity a decade ago and now normally in the charge of a single member of staff.

When I was Holiday Correspondent of *The Western Morning News* in the late 1950s and early 1960s, it was customary to say as much if not more about congestion on rails as on the roads; and indeed more people were usually involved directly and indirectly (such as hoteliers, cafe proprietors and taxi drivers waiting for late trains to bring their customers). Today it is the Exeter bypass and the other inadequacies of the road system that receive the attention and while we build new roads the railways are no longer fully pressed even at the season's height. Yet it should always be remembered that it was the railways that brought first the few wealthy and later the crowds of visitors to the resorts, and that it was indeed as late as the mid-1950s before the trains disgorged their largest loads. Not a single large resort has been created by the motor age which has merely rounded off the development undertaken by the GWR and Southern.

1. Whiteball Summit. 6813 *Eastbury Grange* on the 8.6 Sheffield-Kingswear passes a crowded up train on 7 August 1954. 5157 is the bank engine in the loop, waiting to get back to Wellington

2 Between Taunton and Paddington. 6025 *King Henry III* climbs Brewham bank with the 8.20 Penzance-Paddington in August 1956

3   Between Taunton and Paddington. Another 'King' crosses the Kennet & Avon Canal at Savernake on 17 August 1957. The train is the 8.15 Perranporth-Paddington with 14 typically mixed coaches

4   The 12.15 Kingswear-Wolverhampton on the up relief line at Creech troughs in 1953, as a stopping train from Yeovil approaches Creech St Michael Halt. The express engine is 4960 *Pyle Hall*

5 27 July 1957 at Whiteball. 6915 *Mursley Hall* on the 8.5 Cardiff-Kingswear

6 27 July 1957 at Whiteball. The 7.25 Ealing Broadway-Penzance is about two hours late, headed by 5987 *Brocket Hall*

7   27 July 1957 at Whiteball. As Whiteball down starter signal returns to 'on', 6027 *King Richard I* thunders past with the 9.20 St Ives–Paddington

8　27 July 1957 at Whiteball. 5341 at the end of a slow climb with the heavy 12.5 Paignton-Cardiff, as trains pile up behind

9 Taunton, 5.58pm on 3 August 1957. Seven minutes late, whistle open, 5078 *Beaufort* raises the dust with the 3.20pm Paddington to Kingswear. On the down relief line 3846 stands with a parcels train

10 5005 *Manorbier Castle* speeds through Exeter St David's with the 8.17am Carmarthen to Penzance on 3 August 1957. 32124 is standing on the banker spur and through the arch of the old goods shed can be seen the tender of the standby engine for the day

11   6025 *King Henry III* with the 12.30pm Newquay to Paddington and a clear road signalled ahead, makes an unscheduled four minute stop for water at Exeter St David's on 3 August 1957. On the banker spur at the east end is 32697, while

12 Exeter St David's, 1.50pm on 9 August 1958. 34061 *73 Squadron* having arrived on time with the 12.0 noon Ilfracombe to Waterloo, is delayed five minutes in order to give a clear road to the down *Cornish Riviera Express* headed by 6012 *King Edward VI* coming past at speed on the down through line. This train, in turn, has been delayed by the late running of the 12.15pm all stations from Taunton to Exeter, which has only just arrived in Platform 1 behind 4117

13   On 26 July 1958, 6351 proudly heads *The Devonian*, 9.5am Bradford to Paignton, through the reverse curves at Powderham and along the Exe estuary to Starcross. The passengers' view of the grounds of Powderham Castle is

14   *5067 St Fagans Castle*   leaving Dawlish with the 7.43am Nottingham to Plymouth on 13 July 1957

15 Newton Abbot, 4.7pm on 27 July 1957. 70024 *Vulcan* and 6018 *King Henry VI* leave on the 166 minute late 9.30am Paddington to Newquay from the down through road. At platforms 3/4, 7901 *Dodington Hall* (107) stands on the 7.30am Paddington to Kingswear, while three coaches are detached. 6015 *King Richard III* has already left the 8.50am Paddington to Paignton at platforms 1/2, to be replaced after 15 minutes by 5934 *Kneller Hall* and 6904 *Charfield*

16 Saving a path on the branch, 2211 returns from Kingswear still carrying the stopping passenger headcode from its down working that morning. It is passing Aller Junction coupled ahead of 4967 *Shirenewton Hall* on the 1.40pm Kingswear to Paddington on 13 July 1957

17   With a lighter load than usual on a Saturday, 4922 *Enville Hall* pulls past the Torre advanced starter with a relief to the 8am Kingswear to Paddington on 13 July 1957

18 3796 is assisting the 8.52am Paignton to Leeds, headed by 4079 *Pendennis Castle*, up the 1 in 55 out of Torquay on 3 August 1957, leaving a crowded platform to fill the following 9.5am Paignton to Manchester (London Road) which will be banked by 4606

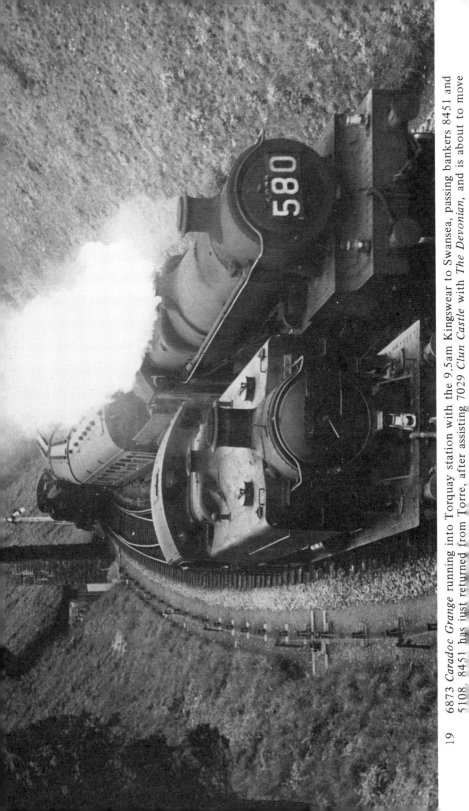

19   6873 *Caradoc Grange* running into Torquay station with the 9.5am Kingswear to Swansea, passing bankers 8451 and 5108. 8451 has just returned from Torre, after assisting 7029 *Clun Castle* with *The Devonian*, and is about to move

20 6860 *Aberporth Grange* and 4928 *Gatacre Hall* with the *Cornish Riviera Express*, approaching Tigley signal box, on the steepest part of Rattery Bank out of Totnes. 24 August 1957

21   A storm broods on the edge of Dartmoor, as 6908 *Downham Hall* and 1021 *County of Montgomery* take the 11.5am Paddington to Penzance up to the South Devon main line summit at Wrangaton on 16 August 1958. The 14 coaches are almost all pre-war GWR stock, with the restaurant car third from the end, to be detached at Plymouth

22 6855 *Saighton Grange* and 5336 seem to have had no trouble lifting the 8.15am Perranporth to Paddington up the stiff climb from Bodmin Road and through Doublebois, on 2 August 1958. At this time, Doublebois station still displayed a 'Cornwall Railway' notice, to be seen on the up side station building, on the right hand edge of the picture

PART TWO
1957

Introduction

This is a description of traffic conditions on the West of England line of the Western Region on Saturday 27 July 1957, particularly the Exeter District stretching from Taunton to Newton Abbot and the Kingswear branch. 1957 was the last year of one hundred per cent steam haulage of main line trains on the Western Region. 27 July 1957 is generally agreed to have been the most chaotic day ever in the West of England, and the volume of traffic on that day has already been described.

In order to investigate the frequent severe delays between Taunton and Newton Abbot on summer Saturdays, a traffic survey was organised by enthusiasts in the area and carried out on 10 August 1957, the peak day for return holiday traffic. No survey was organised on 27 July; the information has been collected from records which have come to light subsequently. The principal observation points were:

Theale	Dawlish
Wellington	Newton Abbot
Exeter St David's	Plymouth

Further information has come from Paddington, Savernake and Southampton Central, and from observers travelling to and from their destinations.

On 27 July 1957, 80 down passenger trains arrived at Newton Abbot between 8.24 am and 9.37 pm. Their average arrival was 122 minutes late. Between 1.15 and 5.15 pm every train arrival exceeded 2 hours late. The worst was the 9.5 Birkenhead-Plymouth, just under 4 hours late. At Exeter the 10.35 Waterloo-Padstow reached St David's before the 8.50 Paddington, and the 11.0 Waterloo-Ilfracombe *Atlantic Coast Express* got there nearly two hours before the 11.0 Paddington.

The chief delays to trains to and from the West of England in steam days almost always occurred on the stretch of line between Taunton and Newton Abbot. At Cogload, near Taunton, the line from Paddington meets the Bristol line, which itself carried four streams of traffic towards the West: the WR route from the Midlands; the LMR route from the Midlands and North; the WR route from the North via Hereford and the Severn Tunnel; and the South Wales trains. All this traffic was carried over the 51 mile stretch of predominantly double track to Newton Abbot, where, at Aller

Junction, the two streams of Plymouth and Torbay traffic diverge. From the flying junction at Cogload there are four tracks through Taunton to Norton Fitzwarren, junction for the branch lines to Minehead and Ilfracombe. Shortly after Norton Fitzwarren is the Wellington bank; here the line climbs for over three miles at 1 in 80/90 to the summit at Whiteball tunnel in the Blackdown hills; on the other side the line is downhill all the way to Exeter St David's, at an easier gradient.

On an ordinary 1957 summer Saturday 38 trains were scheduled to pass Whiteball summit between 10.0 am and 4.0 pm. On 27 July the number was increased to 48, an average of one every 7½ minutes. One of these was a relief running at point-to-point times, no path being available. Although banking engines were provided at Wellington, no provision was made in the working timetable or special traffic notices for trains stopping for a banker; nor for paths for returning bankers, which added to the delays to up traffic. Maximum loads were laid down for the section from Wellington to Whiteball (eg 'Castle' class 450 tons; 'Hall' class 420 tons; 43XX Mogul 394 tons): on 1957 summer Saturdays, these restrictions were sometimes overlooked, and it appeared to be left to the driver's discretion whether or not to request assistance.

Five stations between Norton Fitzwarren and Exeter had platform lines where local trains could be overtaken. In fact on 1957 summer Saturdays only one stopping train left Taunton for Exeter between 9.0 and 4.30, and that was at 12.15. In the up direction the service was almost identical.

Numerous holiday expresses in both directions were booked to be overtaken at Exeter. The line is shared with the SR West of England main line on the 1¼ mile stretch between Cowley Bridge Junction and Exeter St David's, the SR trains running in the opposite direction to the WR ones. In practice WR trains suffered few delays from this quarter.

From Exeter the line follows the Exe estuary to Dawlish Warren, runs along the coast to Teignmouth, and then up the Teign estuary to Newton Abbot. On this stretch of line no local stopping trains ran on 1957 summer Saturdays in either direction between 9.30 and 4.0, but a large proportion of the expresses called at Dawlish and Teignmouth and some made further stops. For example, the Saturday 6.40 am from Leicester ran in the timings of a regular stopping train from Exeter to Paignton.

Newton Abbot is the junction station for the Kingswear branch, where most of the holiday traffic is bound for, although the junction itself is at Aller, one mile further west. Four tracks exist between these points, and although the two tracks in each direction can be used by trains for either Plymouth or Kingswear, generally Plymouth trains are routed on the main lines and branch trains on the relief. The present Newton Abbot station was completed in 1927 and consists of two spacious island platforms, with a through road in each direction for non-stop trains. The outer face of each platform is connected to the through road by a scissors crossing half way along the platform, which helps the dividing or joining of trains with branch portions, and enables the branch portion of a down train to leave first if necessary. The east and west halves of each road are separately signalled, so that in theory the station could accommodate twelve trains at once, provided each was limited to 9 or 10 coaches; in practice this facility was not often used with normal through trains, and was usually restricted to the acceptance of terminating local trains, which could thus enter the station while another train was at the front end of the platform. A less safety conscious railway than the GWR (and its successor) might have made greater use of it: when trains made long stops at Newton Abbot (such as the parcels train, which, as we shall see, caused so much congestion in the middle of the day), following trains, although calling at the station, could then have used the scissors crossover in order to overtake.

At Newton Abbot nearly all expresses for the Plymouth line took on pilot engines for the South Devon banks. The pilots were mainly of the 'Grange', 'Manor' or 41XX classes. Larger engines of all types took their turn as pilots, incorporated in main line duties. If the pilot was an engine with a pony truck leading instead of a bogie (eg, a 41XX tank), it was supposed to be coupled inside the train engine if going beyond Brent, but could be coupled ahead if detached there. A pair of two-cylinder engines invariably took over the down *Cornish Riviera Express* on summer Saturdays from the 'King' which had worked it from Paddington. The Saturday 'Limited', carrying a main portion for St Ives, then ran non-stop through Plymouth to Truro. Its 'King' locomotive was immediately attached in front of the engine of the 10.35 Paddington-Penzance, usually another 'King', and the two engines worked together as far as Plymouth.

Another summer Saturday locomotive procedure at Newton Abbot concerned trains destined for Paignton. From the early morning until mid-afternoon a stream of trains departed from Paignton to all parts of the country. Until the early afternoon nearly all down trains terminating at Paignton changed engines at Newton Abbot, and were worked down the branch by an engine running tender first, which had already been serviced and prepared for a specific up departure from Paignton.

In the whole of a summer Saturday only five down trains were scheduled to pass through Newton Abbot without stopping.

A few engines worked through to Paignton and returned to Newton Abbot shortly afterwards on an up train tender first; two such up trains were the 2.55 and 3.10 Paignton-Wolverhampton, which thus changed engines at Newton Abbot. Other engines working through to Paignton returned light direct to Newton Abbot, leaving their stock to be stored or reformed at Paignton.

The empty stock of relief trains with no booked return working was either worked back empty to Torre for disposal in the up goods yard – up to three 10-coach trains could be left here, provided the coal wagons had been cleared away on the Friday evening – or else taken through to Newton Abbot or beyond for disposal. As will be seen later, it is possible that some of these ECS workings in the up direction were partly responsible for the delays to trains leaving the Kingswear branch; but their working would have been essential, in order to relieve congestion at Paignton.

As far back as 1935 it was recognised that the layout at Paignton was inadequate for the summer traffic, and plans were passed for the reconstruction of the station on a higher level, to eliminate the very busy level crossings at each end of the station: also for the reconstruction of Goodrington Sands Halt, ¾ mile west of Paignton, to eliminate a further busy level crossing, and to provide additional sorely needed carriage sidings and a locomotive turntable and servicing facilities on reclaimed land alongside the halt. By 1957 the latter part of the scheme had just been completed: the plans for the rebuilding of Paignton station itself not having been revived after the war, this remained as it was, the level crossings now busier than ever.

Consequently, on peak Saturdays such as 27 July 1957 it was only by exercising considerable ingenuity that the staff were able to cope with the volume of traffic arriving on the still very limited siding capacity available to them. By late Saturday evening every available length of track would be occupied by coaching stock, some sets being broken down in order to fit them into the goods shed and coal sidings.

The new turntable at Goodrington, although operational, was apparently used by only four engines during the day. It would seem therefore that the timetable planners had not yet adjusted the locomotive workings to make full use of it. In subsequent years much greater use was made of this facility, thus doing away with much of the engine changing which took place at Newton Abbot in 1957, and some of the consequent delay.

During the period of observation on 27 July 1957 72 down trains made scheduled calls at Newton Abbot. They lost an average of 4.8 minutes in the station. It was not unusual for the majority of trains to outstay their booked time at Newton Abbot on a summer Saturday. One of the main reasons for this has already been discussed. Another was the shortage of crews caused by late running. A train might arrive at Newton Abbot after the time at which the engine crew or guard should have signed off, having worked to Paignton and back, and a substitute crew might have to be found to take the train forward. Some crews might not know the road to Paignton in any event, and a pilotman would be required.

Down Trains

When the Dawlish observer, on holiday from Birmingham, arrived on the scene shortly after six in the morning, the down overnight trains were running up to two hours late. This was not unusual for a peak summer Saturday in the 1950s, and local opinion has it that the probable cause was the programming of more trains over the section west of Taunton, in particular the Wellington bank, than could realistically be handled. On 27 July 1957, with a number of extras running, 48 down trains were booked to pass Whiteball tunnel between midnight and 7.0 am, an average of one every 8¾ minutes. These included 14 relief trains from the Birmingham area in connection with the industrial holidays. As already stated, no allowance was made in the timetable for stops for banking assistance at Wellington, although this was available and often necessary

with the heavy loads of a 1957 summer Saturday. The progress of
these trains would be further hampered by the longer block sections
existing at night: nine signal boxes between Taunton and Newton
Abbot were switched out for the night shift.

Between 8.0 and 9.0 trains were losing 15-20 minutes between
Dawlish and Newton Abbot, and most were exceeding their allowance at the latter station. Torquay branch trains changing engines
at Newton Abbot were probably delayed by the disorganisation
of the locomotive workings. It is known that on several occasions
later in the day engines were sent down from Newton Abbot to
Paignton ahead of their normal working, in order to cause less
delay to their designated up departures. If this also happened on
some of the overnight trains, delay would be caused while Newton
Abbot found a fresh engine. Four trains changing engines at Newton Abbot between 8.40 and 9.47 spent 17, 16, 30 and 15 minutes
in the station. While the 10.10 pm Hull-Paignton was in the station
from 9.20 to 9.50, there was effectively only one other down line
in use, because all following trains were booked to make passenger
stops. Both the 10.30 pm Manchester-Paignton and 11.35 pm Liverpool-Penzance had vehicles detached at Newton Abbot, and so the
platforms were occupied even longer after the trains had departed.
The 10.10 Hull was overtaken by two trains not changing engines,
and may have been delayed by the need to find a scratch crew for
6904 *Charfield Hall,* as the engine workings for up trains at this
time of the day had evidently departed from normal.

1000 *County of Middlesex* on the 5.30 pm Glasgow took twelve
coaches to Plymouth unassisted.

The 7-coach train, hauled by 1009 *County of Carmarthen* (82A),
carried 'Paddington Bath Spa and Bristol' roof boards, and these
may have been a scratch set put on by Temple Meads at the last
minute. If so, it was partly a relief to the 11.35 pm Liverpool-
Penzance, and partly a substitute for the very late-running 12.25
am Manchester-Plymouth. After arrival at Plymouth 1009 did take
up the return working of the 12.25 Manchester on the 10.45
Penzance-Sheffield.

Another train identification query concerns the 11.10 pm and
12.8 am Manchester-Paignton. According to the reporting numbers
the 12.8 was running ahead of the 11.10 and reached Newton
Abbot only 33 minutes late. It was not observed at Exeter and so

must have left there within a few minutes of its scheduled departure at 8.27. Other indications, however, suggest that these two Manchester trains were carrying the wrong reporting numbers. Apart from the greater probability of their running in the correct order, the engine of the 12.8 Manchester, based at Shrewsbury, was booked to work through to Paignton, and later take over the 3.10 Paignton-Wolverhampton at Newton Abbot. When the second train reached Newton Abbot at 12.18, 5968 *Cory Hall* (84G) was replaced by 4150, and later took over the 3.10 Paignton. This looks like an unscheduled move by Newton Abbot to ensure that the 'Hall' was ready to take up its return working, by replacing it with a spare tank engine. Also the stock of the 12.8 am Manchester was booked to return on the 12.5 Paignton-Cardiff. If the 12.8 reached Paignton only 30-40 minutes late there would be nothing to explain the delay to the 12.5 up, 27 minutes late at Newton Abbot. Its locomotive, 5341, must have got down in fairly good time on the 6.5 Cardiff-Paignton, and up branch trains which were not delayed by late arrival of engine or stock were reaching Newton Abbot close to time. Circumstances tend to suggest that the 12.5 Paignton's departure was delayed by reason of its stock not yet having arrived at Paignton, and a substitute rake having to be found.

Even if down overnight trains were arriving late, there should normally have been time for recovery before the main stream of the day trains began to arrive. Between 9.35 and 10.31 only two trains were due to arrive at Newton Abbot. On this occasion, however, overnight trains were still arriving without respite until 10.7. Times recorded at Exeter St David's (except for departures between 1.57 and 5.40) are approximate, but it now becomes possible to see how much time was being lost between Exeter and Newton Abbot.

While the stream of overnight trains was occupying the down platforms at Newton Abbot, the 9.32 local to Paignton, hauled by 5011 *Tintagel Castle* tender first, departed direct from the carriage sidings at 9.55, without entering a platform, and carrying class C headlamps.

The 9.30 Exeter-Kingswear all stations, with 3677 and 9 non-corridors, lost about 25 minutes between Exeter and Newton Abbot, despite an apparently clear road as the previous train had arrived at Newton Abbot 32 minutes earlier. Then, although the train was full, three coaches were removed. This train had a note in the working notice to the effect that it was not to be sidetracked for express trains running out of course. However, it is clear that after arrival at Newton Abbot it must have taken over an hour to get to Torquay.

This was probably due to a combination of two factors. Firstly, as has already been explained, at times of pressure the layout at Paignton made it extremely difficult to dispose of the stock of the succession of trains terminating there, and banking engines returning from Torre to Torquay added to the congestion on the down line. On 27 July 1957 eight trains left Newton Abbot for Paignton between 9.0 and 10.30; all but one were to terminate there.

The other cause of delay on the branch was the 10.50 Newton Abbot-Torquay empty stock, which had departed on time and was next in front of the Exeter local. This was the engine, tender first, and the stock for the 11.30 Torquay-Paddington; at Torquay the engine had to draw the train into the up platform, via the special facing points at the eastern end of the station, and run round. Because of the congestion on the down line already described, it is not known how long the empty train took to reach the outskirts of Torquay. But the 10.35 Torquay-Paddington and 10.35 Paignton-Wolverhampton could not have left Torquay until nearly 12.0 and the stock for the 11.30 Torquay could not have cleared the down line until these two up trains had been dealt with, as of course it followed them at Newton Abbot. It seems quite likely, therefore, that the empty train was held outside Torquay blocking the down line for anything up to half an hour.

The 6.10 Kidderminster-Paignton relief, which followed the Exeter local, must also have been delayed; after that 55 minutes elapsed before the next train left for the branch at 12.20, giving Paignton a chance to recover before the morning departures from London, the Midlands and South Wales started to arrive.

On the main line things nearly got back to normal. The packed 6.55 Paddington-Penzance took just over half an hour between Exeter and Newton Abbot, while the 6.10 Kidderminster regained time, covering the 8 miles from Dawlish in 10 minutes. Time was being lost only between Exeter and Dawlish.

There was then a gap of 36 minutes before the next train arrived at Newton Abbot, and it is this holdup, during a period when trains should have been arriving continuously, that seems to have started the really serious delays which persisted for the rest of the day. Between 11.0 and 12.0 only three trains arrived at Newton Abbot, compared with nine scheduled. The train in question was 6824 *Ashley Grange* hauling the 13-coach 7.0 Swindon-Penzance; it lost over thirty minutes between Exeter and Newton Abbot and, with two intermediate stops, took 34 minutes longer over the journey than the 6.10 Kidderminster-Paignton which had overtaken it at Exeter. After this trains began to reach Newton Abbot in the region of an hour late. The slow running of the Swindon may have been due to its 'Grange' struggling with a heavy load, but more probably was caused by the long parcels train hauled by 3850, which left Exeter (Riverside) ahead of the 6.10 Kidderminster, and must have been side-tracked more than once on the way to Newton Abbot. This train may have let the Kidderminster past at Exminster and then delayed the 7.0 Swindon from there on to Dawlish Warren. Because of its 86E engine the parcels train has been identified as the 7.55 pm Cardiff-Plymouth, in which case it left Exeter 576 minutes late, but it may have been the 10.40 pm from Paddington via Bristol (due to call at Newton Abbot 8.15/8.45 but not observed) or a combination of the two.

After the arrival at Newton Abbot of the 7.0 Swindon at 11.52, there was absolutely no respite in the arrivals of down trains until the last observer left after 9.30 pm. Delays grew worse and worse until the majority of arrivals were between two and three hours late. There was little opportunity to regain time: of the twelve passenger train arrivals in the first two hours after 11.52, two were overnight trains running well out of course, five were relief trains and only five regular trains. At 11.51½, on the 20 mile section between Exeter and Newton Abbot, containing 13 intermediate block posts, there were 10 trains which lost an average of 32 minutes.

An observer from Newton Abbot travelled to Plymouth on the 7.0 Swindon-Penzance, and it can be seen that by comparison virtually no time was being lost over the South Devon banks. In fact the two 'Castles' on the 9.35 Bristol-Penzance regained 10 minutes, taking only 10 minutes longer with two stops than the non-stop schedule of the Monday to Friday *Limited* in those days. The Swindon spent 24 minutes at Plymouth changing engines. The 'Manor' and the 'Grange' came off separately, and the two engines which replaced them came on separately too.

In the mean time incidents on the Exeter-Newton Abbot section combined to aggravate the delays in that area. The 12.8 am Manchester-Paignton, making an unscheduled engine change as already referred to, spent 13 minutes at Newton Abbot. The 7.0 and 7.5 Paddington were carrying the wrong reporting numbers, the locomotives evidently having backed on to the wrong trains at Paddington. The 7.0 was a relief to Newton Abbot booked to call only at Dawlish, but in fact called at Exeter; the regular train, whose departure had been put back five minutes to 7.5, failed to make its booked stop at Exeter and ran through to Dawlish non-stop. It left Newton Abbot crowded with passengers from the relief train.

A major contributor to the delays at this time was the parcels train which arrived at Newton Abbot at 12.46 and occupied one of the platforms for no less than 62 minutes while vans were detached. During this period only five other trains were dealt with, and at 1.45 yet another local train, the 12.30 to Plymouth, departed direct from the carriage sidings without entering a platform, taking with it several vans off the parcels train which was still in the station. The following table shows how trains must have queued up to use the remaining platform or the through line:

Platforms 1/2	*Platforms 3/4*	*Through Road*
Parcels	8.10 Newport	9.35 Bristol
12.46/1.48	12.58/1.18	12.53/12.59
		9.40 Bristol
		1.6/1.13
	12.25 Manchester	
	1.22/1.38	
	7.0 Birmingham	
	1.44/2.15	
8.23 Reading		
1.52/2.3		
7.20 Birmingham		
2.10/2.23		
	8.5 Cardiff	
	2.23/2.31	

The two Bristol trains were the only ones not making advertised stops at Newton Abbot. Thus it is fairly obvious that the 7.0 Birmingham-Penzance waited about 17 minutes for a platform, as it could not use the through road. It arrived in the adjacent platform just before the parcels left, and it was 31 minutes before that platform was cleared. Between 1.0 and 2.0 only four trains arrived at Newton Abbot as against seven scheduled, and they had lost an average of 43 minutes from Exeter alone. At times the holdup in the Newton Abbot area reacted almost back to Exeter.

The 7.0 Birmingham conveyed a 5-coach rear portion for Paignton, scheduled to work forward at 11.55 with the engine for the 1.55 Paignton-Wolverhampton. When the' 7.0 eventually reached Newton Abbot at 1.44, the Paignton portion was terminated, although not removed from the platform until 2.15. The engine concerned, 5939 *Tangley Hall,* had departed for the branch at 1.37 running light! Even so the 1.55 Paignton passed Newton Abbot 34 minutes late.

Following the Birmingham was the 8.23 Reading-Paignton, a relief to the 7.25 Ealing Broadway-Penzance. This train was booked to run at point-to-point times in the Exeter Division, which meant that no pathway was available for it.

The Cardiff parcels must have been passed by the 7.0 Birmingham before Aller Junction. There was then a gap of 67 minutes before the next train left Newton Abbot for the Plymouth line, and so the parcels caused no further delay.

The 13-coach 8.5 Cardiff-Kingswear began its journey in the hands of 43XX 2-6-0 7322. It had a completely unchecked run as far as Bristol, even through the Severn Tunnel, but lost 21 minutes. Time was outstayed at all stations owing to overcrowding, and a large number of passengers were actually left behind at Severn Tunnel Junction. A 61XX tank had to be taken as pilot through the Severn Tunnel, necessitating an unscheduled stop at Filton Junction to detach. Because this train was allowed 30 minutes at Bristol, departure behind 6915 *Mursley Hall* was only 4 minutes late. When next observed at Exeter the 8.5 Cardiff was 1½ hours behind time; it left Exeter at 1.0 and was overtaken, presumably at Dawlish Warren, by the 7.20 Birmingham (New Street) -Paignton relief which had left Temple Meads 16 minutes later. This suggests that the Cardiff may have been ordered to make additional stops at St Thomas and Dawlish Warren in the path of the 6.40 Leicester-Paignton which should have left Exeter at 1.0.

Between 2.0 and 3.0 only five trains arrived at Newton Abbot instead of nine booked; these had lost an average of 40 minutes from Exeter. The 8.10 Paddington-Paignton spent 11 minutes at Newton Abbot changing engines: it took an unscheduled pilot, 5067 *St Fagan's Castle,* which was due to work the 2.45 Paignton-Paddington and should have gone down on the 8.50 Paddington. However, the 8.10 itself did not leave Newton Abbot until 2.41.

The 8.25 Paddington to Penzance and Perranporth, headed by 5055 *Earl of Eldon,* was the one train in the early afternoon which could have alleviated the pressure on Newton Abbot's two down platforms by stopping on the through line to attach its pilot engine, since the train was advertised non-stop from Paddington to Brent. Instead the 8.25 drew into platforms 3 and 4, which suggests that it may have been ordered to stop specially for the numerous Cornish passengers who must have been waiting at Newton Abbot at this time. The train which terminated at Newton Abbot in front of the 8.25 was the first of three portions of the 6.55 Wolverhampton-Paignton, itself a Saturday extra.

After 3.0 some of the trains arriving at Newton Abbot had lost 50 minutes or more from Exeter. At 3.53½, and again at 4.17, this stretch of line was occupied block-and-block with 12 trains.

The 7.25 Ealing Broadway-Penzance was already an hour late in the London Division and was behind three Paddington trains, the 8.10, 8.20 to Weymouth Quay, and 8.25, which it should have preceded. It is unlikely to have been delayed by its relief, which originated at Reading; but it is possible that it reached Reading on the relief line only about 30 minutes late but was held for the three Paddington trains which passed through non-stop. The 7.25 Ealing stopped at Newbury, and the 8.0 Reading-Bristol stopping train was booked to shunt for it to get past. But on this occasion the stopping train was noted ahead of the 7.25 at Savernake, and may have caused further delay between Newbury and Patney & Chirton, although the interval between them is not known. It would be a serious matter for an express which got behind a stopping train on this section. The 8.0 Reading was scheduled to take 23 minutes longer between Newbury and Patney than the 7.25 Ealing.

The 7.25 Ealing had a corridor refreshment service. It reached Taunton at the same time as the 7.30 Paddington which had come via Bristol. Between Creech Junction and Taunton the two trains ran neck and neck, stopping at every signal, and pies were sold through the window to the passengers on the 7.30 Paddington.

When times in the Bristol district are known for some trains, it becomes obvious that, besides Newton Abbot, another area further east is causing heavy delays. The departure of the 9.35 and 9.40 Bristol-Penzance was recorded by the observer on his way from Cardiff to Wellington. They lost 40 to 50 minutes between Bristol and Exeter, a distance of 75½ miles. The 7.0 Birmingham lost an hour from St Philip's Marsh. The situation deteriorated still further: the 7.30 Birmingham (Moor Street) and the 6.55 Wolverhampton-Paignton took between 3½ and 4 hours for the 75½ miles.

The Wellington observer had planned to leave Bristol on the 6.35 Walsall-Kingswear, but it was so crowded that there was no standing window space, and so he waited for the 7.30 Paddington-Kingswear. This train did not do badly between Bristol and Taunton, comparatively speaking. It lost 21 minutes on this section, and it reached Taunton 28 minutes late on a revised schedule. There were checks as far as South Liberty Junction: then 7901 *Dodington Hall* made 60 mph through Yatton. There was a 6 minute signal stand at Uphill Junction, but no more checks until the approaches to Taunton. The 7.30 was evidently side-tracked at Dawlish Warren, although not booked to call there, to allow the 9.30 Paddington-Newquay past, and so lost 29 minutes between Exeter and Dawlish alone. The 9.30 was supposed to have overtaken it at Norton Fitzwarren on this day. Then the 7.30 waited 20 minutes at Newton Abbot, although not changing engines, presumably to allow the 8.50 Paddington to get ahead. The 8.50 should have been ahead all the way from Cogload, and its locomotives and coaching stock were due to leave Paignton within a matter of minutes as the 4.15 to Paddington.

The 8.50 Paddington-Paignton, a 14-coach load hauled by 6015 *King Richard III,* was 12 minutes late at Theale. It was close behind the 8.30 Paddington-Weymouth Quay, which itself was following the 7.25 Ealing Broadway. The 8.30 was timed 7 minutes slower from Reading to Castle Cary than the 8.50, mainly because of a stop at Heywood Road Junction to reman. They were still behind the 7.25 Ealing at Savernake, despite the 7.25's Newbury stop. The 8.50 trailed the 7.25 into Taunton, having lost 39 minutes from Theale; it then took over two hours to reach Exeter, a loss of 75 minutes on schedule and an average speed of 15 mph. The 8.50 lost a further 41 minutes to Newton Abbot and then spent 15 minutes at that station, probably because its rostered engine had already gone down on the 8.10.

At 12.35 there were 13 trains between Taunton and Exeter, when there should have been 6 according to the special traffic notice. This works out at one for every $2\frac{1}{3}$ miles. Looking at the situation as a whole during the midday rush, the few trains seen at Taunton itself had lost a considerable amount of time already by this point, the 7.30 Paddington having had a better than average run from Bristol. Much of the loss would appear to have been in the approaches to Taunton. The observation of the down *Limited* at Fairwood Junction, near Westbury, shows that of the 77 minutes lost by this train between Theale and Wellington all but 8 were lost west of Fairwood Junction.

By comparing the few Taunton times with the Wellington times, although trains were not observed at both points, it can be seen that relatively little time was lost between Wellington and Exeter. The 10.35 Paddington-Penzance lost only 10 minutes between these points, and the 8.17 Carmarthen-Penzance only 3 minutes. Yet the five expresses seen at both Taunton and Exeter all lost between 64 and 75 minutes on this section.

By midday and for the rest of the afternoon the main point of delay seems to have been just west of Taunton. There was the bottleneck at Norton Fitzwarren, where four tracks merge into two, and just over five miles further on Wellington bank begins in earnest. The time taken by trains to surmount this barrier must have caused those behind to be held at both Victory Siding and Poole Siding, the two block posts in between, and on such a day a double line of trains would be creeping forward to the signalbox at Norton Fitzwarren and a single line from there on to Wellington. The queue could stretch back beyond Taunton, thus explaining the delays east of that point. It should be remembered that all the trains for the Minehead and Ilfracombe branches also had to use the Taunton-Norton Fitzwarren section.

The times recorded at Wellington are of each train as it crawled through the station, until 4.0 pm when they began stopping in the station. Every down train seen there (ie from 2.0 to 6.0 pm) was halted at the advanced starter signal.

Although there is an intermediate block section on the down line between Wellington and Whiteball, half-way up the bank, even so, once the trains have lost their momentum, the sections on the bank are too long to enable the booked headway of 6 or 7 minutes to be maintained. Once one train has been slowed, or stopped, at Wellington, the next loses its chance of a run at the bank, and succeeding trains are delayed more and more. This process goes on until there is a timetable path with no train to fill it, enabling all those behind to catch up by 7 minutes.

On 27 July 1957 trains were being scheduled over Whiteball summit at 6½ minute intervals from 9.40 to 12.5. During this time, not only were there no blank paths, but there was one relief train scheduled with no path for it and shown in the special traffic notice as running at point-to-point times. This meant that even in ideal circumstances all those trains unfortunate enough to be behind it were certain to be a few minutes late, until a blank path occurred. In practice, with this density of traffic, the timetable headway became unattainable. This was because engine power frequently did not match train load, and while a 'Castle' on 8 coaches might sprint up the bank, it was quite likely that the next train, perhaps with a South Wales 'Mogul' struggling at the head of 13 packed corridors, would take as much as 20 minutes to reach the summit.

Beyond Whiteball there is a downhill run all the way to Exeter; with 10-15 minutes on average being taken on the climb, as each train breasted the summit it probably had three or four block sections clear ahead, which would explain why so little time was lost on to Exeter. Any loss between Wellington and Exeter was probably all on the bank itself.

According to the timetable the intensity of the down service slackened off after 3.0 pm to only five trains an hour at Taunton, and after 5.0 pm to only three an hour. But on 27 July 1957 trains were still reaching Taunton in a steady stream up to 6.30 pm, and the stretch of line to Wellington never had time to recover from the delays. The Wellington observer returned to Taunton about 6.0 pm by a local service, and on the 7 mile journey passed 6 down trains, most of which were in a queue at Norton Fitzwarren. The Dawlish observer followed shortly afterwards travelling on the 3.10 Paignton-Wolverhampton. At 6.40 he passed 4 down trains in 2 minutes near Norton Fitzwarren. The 9.25 Bradford-Paignton left Taunton at 6.25, but had not reached Norton Fitzwarren, two miles away, by 6.40.

The progress of the 12.15 Taunton-Exeter brings the extent of the delays in the Taunton area into high relief; it was the only train with a recorded time at both Taunton and Wellington, being used by the observer from Cardiff on the final stage of his journey. The 12.15 was held back at Taunton so as to depart in its correct sequence in the procession of expresses, and therefore left at 1.5. It then took no less than 58 minutes to reach Wellington, a journey scheduled at 10 minutes; and this journey was typical of the day, in that the local used the relief line as far as Norton Fitzwarren, and the 9.30 and 9.40 Paddington were passed and repassed several times, but no express was given priority. On the contrary, the 9.40 did not overtake the local at Wellington as booked, perhaps because a stopping train could make almost as good time to Exeter in the prevailing conditions. Thus the 12.15 Taunton was 98 minutes late at Wellington, but only lost two more minutes to Exeter. It probably delayed the 9.40 by 10-15 minutes.

The loss of time of the 9.30 Paddington-Newquay between the six observation points was as follows:

Minutes
44
64
21
14 (+ 16 minutes lost at Newton Abbot)
7

Nevertheless it had quite a good run relatively to other trains: it got ahead of the 6.40 Leicester before Norton Fitzwarren, overtook at Exeter the 8.50 Paddington which it should have followed to Newton Abbot, and passed the 7.30 Paddington before Newton Abbot. The delay at Newton Abbot may have been caused by awaiting a pilot: 70024 *Vulcan* had only come off the 6.35 Walsall 28 minutes earlier.

At 4.0 there were three down trains stationary at Newton Abbot, two of which stayed there for 20 minutes and one 15 minutes. This undoubtedly delayed the 6.40 Leicester-Paignton and 9.40 Paddington-Paignton. The 10.20 Paddington-Kingswear, one of only two down trains to pass non-stop through Newton Abbot on that day, could have used the through line after the departure of the 9.30 at 4.6, but that it was behind two trains which had to make passenger stops at Newton Abbot, and neither of these could enter until after 4.12 as both platforms were occupied. The eight trains which arrived at Newton Abbot between 3.0 and 4.0 had lost an average of 47 minutes from Exeter: the eight in the next hour improved on that average by one minute.

The 9.40 Paddington-Paignton was booked to overtake the 9.35 Paddington-Minehead while the 9.35 called at Westbury. The 9.40 dropped 95 minutes from Theale to Wellington. The 10.20 Paddington-Kingswear was almost invariably a 'King' or 'Castle' on 13 coaches, and was probably rostered for a 'King'. On this day 7910 *Hown Hall* of Southall shed was used, and the load reduced to 11, perhaps for that reason. 7910 must, however, have been one of the more highly regarded of its class, as on the previous Saturday it had worked the down *Capitals United Express.*

After the 10.20 came the *Limited*, which was one of the trains to lose over 50 minutes between Exeter and Newton Abbot, and then the 10.37 Cardiff-Paignton relief, whose 'Manor' was piloted from Taunton to Exeter by 4979 *Wootton Hall,* the engine of the 9.35 Paddington-Minehead which came off at Taunton. (It was the 10.37 Cardiff which, a fortnight later, with a 43XX 2-6-0 hauling a slightly lighter load, caused heavy delays to the *Limited* and following trains by taking 70 minutes from Taunton to Exeter.)

At 4.55 Newton Abbot established a record for the day: the aggregate amount of time lost in the station by the five trains dealt with since 4.15 was nil. These included the 10.30 and 10.35 Paddington.

The 11.0 Paddington-Penzance and Kingsbridge ran behind the 11.5 Paddington throughout its journey, departure having been delayed by the late arrival of the empty stock at Paddington. The same transposition took place on 26 July 1958. From 10.30 to 11.15 was Paddington's busiest period for departures on summer Saturdays in the 1950s, with a departure every 5 minutes, and on 27 July 1957 there were two reliefs, making a total of 12 departures in 45 minutes. The 11.5 itself, a normal 'Castle' duty headed by 5916 *Trinity Hall*, left Paddington after the 11.10 to Birkenhead and the 11.12 Bristol relief. It was the first train to stop for a banker at Wellington since observation began there at 2.0.

˜ After 5.0 all trains were again exceeding their station times at Newton Abbot. The eight arrivals during the next hour had lost an average of 34 minutes from Exeter, an improvement on the average of the previous four hours. The 9.5 Swansea-Kingswear, although not changing engines, spent 17 minutes in the station; the 8.55 Wolverhampton-Penzance took 19 minutes to attach a pilot, being passed meanwhile by the 9.25 Wolverhampton-Paignton, another packed train which had come via Oxford and Swindon behind 43XX 2-6-0 5385. After the 9.25 came 7004 *Eastnor Castle* on the 14-coach 11.0 Paddington-Penzance, which had also taken assistance on Wellington bank. The 11.0 was not making an advertised stop at Newton Abbot, but was forced to use one of the platforms as the 8.55 Wolverhampton still occupied the through road. As the Wolverhampton train left, the *Torbay Express,* which should have passed through non-stop, pulled up for water. Thus at 5.54 all the down lines at Newton Abbot were occupied by nominal non-stop trains which should have used the through road in succession. This delayed the 8.6 Sheffield-Kingswear, which was making an advertised stop and so had to use a platform road. The Sheffield train called at all stations from Newton Abbot onwards, and was overtaken as booked by the 10.55 Birmingham-Paignton; 6874 *Haughton Grange,* which took over the Sheffield, had arrived at Newton Abbot piloting 70024 *Vulcan* on the 6.35 Walsall-Kingswear.

The 10.35 Wolverhampton-Paignton, which left Exeter at 5.40, was the first train to drop less than 20 minutes to Newton Abbot since the 7.0 Paddington, 6½ hours earlier. With the reduced intensity of traffic, matters continued to improve on this section, and the 8.0 Manchester-Penzance only lost approximately 8 minutes. However, Newton Abbot evidently began to have difficulty in finding pilots or replacement locomotives or crew: from the 8.0 Manchester onwards, all trains (except the 3.30 Paddington-Penzance) were making advertised calls at Newton Abbot, and so there were effectively only two down lines through the station. The Penzance portion of the 8.0 Manchester spent 45 minutes in the station, although the Kingswear portion got away 30 minutes earlier;

the driver of 7019 *Fowey Castle* was waiting for assistance, eventually provided by 4150: with only 9 coaches the need for this may not have been anticipated. An hour later the Kingswear portion of the 9.15 Liverpool spent 41 minutes at the station.

Platform occupation at Newton Abbot between 7.0 and 9.0 pm was as follows:

Platforms 1/2			Platforms 3/4		
8.0	Manchester	6.58/7.43 D	7.45	Rotherham	6.50/6.57
			1.25	Paddington	7.12/7.29
			1.35	Paddington	7.36/7.46
8.45	Liverpool	7.49/8.8 D	7.0	West Hartlepool	7.51/8.11
9.0	Manchester	8.13/8.21	9.15	Liverpool	8.17/8.58 D
9.5	Bradford	8.25/8.33			
7.30	Newcastle	8.39/8.47			
9.5	Birkenhead	8.52/8.57			

D – Train dividing

The *Royal Duchy* was behind the 1.25 Paddington-Kingswear at a time when only one platform was effectively in use, and the 1.25 spent 17 minutes at Newton Abbot. So the *Royal Duchy* lost approximately 31 minutes from Exeter, of which 20 may have been spent waiting outside Newton Abbot. The rear portion of the 1.25 Paddington was labelled for Paignton but was in fact detached at Newton Abbot, perhaps because Paignton was unable to cope with the disposal of any more stock, and the full load of 13 coaches was too much for a 'Hall' to take through to Kingswear. The 7.30 Newcastle-Paignton and 9.5 Birkenhead-Plymouth were also badly hit by these delays, arriving while one platform was occupied by the 9.15 Liverpool, and they lost approximately 31 and 33 minutes from Exeter. The 3.30 Paddington-Penzance managed to overtake the 3.20 Paddington-Kingswear after Exeter, presumably at Dawlish Warren, although the 3.20 was not booked to call there. The 3.30 was booked non-stop from Exeter to Plymouth, while the 3.20 called at Dawlish, Teignmouth and Newton Abbot.

One might have expected the 3.30 to have overtaken the 9.5 Birkenhead by using the through line at Newton Abbot and run ahead of it to Plymouth, since the Birkenhead had to call at Totnes and Brent. Instead the 3.30 did not enter Newton Abbot until the 9.5 Birkenhead had left, and stopped in the platform. The purpose of this was probably to pick up Cornwall passengers on the Birkenhead, who would normally have connected into the 1.35 Paddington at Plymouth, but on this day might otherwise have been stranded. The 3.30 lost approximately 43 minutes between Exeter and Newton Abbot, and the 3.20, which had been sidetracked, 57 minutes. The 9.25 Bradford-Paignton left Exeter a full half-hour after the 3.30 Paddington but nevertheless caught up with the procession before Newton Abbot, and so lost 19 minutes. The 7.15 Exeter-Paignton followed the 9.25 Bradford as booked. Its engine, 7300, had not reached Exeter until approximately 7.15 on the 4.32 Plymouth.

To return finally to the Wellington bank, four trains were banked during the four hours of observation, all of 13 or 14 coaches. The observations at Wellington suggest that severe delays were occurring at Norton Fitzwarren right up to the end of the day. Losses between Wellington and Exeter were not generally more than 20 minutes, but the 9.25 Bradford-Paignton, the only train observed at Taunton at this time of the evening, took approximately 1 hour 55 minutes from Taunton to Exeter, a loss of 74 minutes, and the number of down trains seen near Norton Fitzwarren at this time has already been mentioned. The *Royal Duchy* took on 6926 *Holkham Hall* (84B) as pilot from Taunton, presumably to Plymouth. (On 10 August the previous working of this pilot engine was on the 10.50 Wolverhampton-Minehead.)

The 9.5 Birkenhead-Plymouth should have followed next after the 8.45 Liverpool. Instead it was 173 minutes late when first seen at Wellington, and was behind the 9.15 Liverpool. This delay had presumably occurred somewhere on the North-to-West route, considerably earlier in its journey. At the start of its journey the Birkenhead conveyed a rear portion for Cardiff, which was detached at Pontypool Road.

The 9.5 Bradford-Paignton and 7.30 Newcastle-Paignton carried the wrong reporting numbers. It seems that the wrong locomotives must have backed on to the two trains at Bristol, perhaps because the identity of the trains was confused as they were running in the wrong order. The 9.5 Bradford was the normal return working from Bristol of the engine off the 8.30 Paignton-LMR relief. On this date 6814 *Enbourne Grange* off the 8.30 returned on the Newcastle train, while the Bradford was worked by an engine not previously observed.

The last train observed at Newton Abbot was the 11.45 Manchester-Plymouth, which according to the timetable should have arrived almost an hour after the previous express, the 9.25 Bradford-Paignton. Even at this late hour approximately 20 minutes were lost between Huntspill, near Highbridge, and Exeter, and the 11.45 Manchester drew into Newton Abbot, 69 minutes late, as soon as the Bradford had departed, the other platform still being occupied by the 7.15 Exeter-Paignton.

Time lost by passenger trains between
Exeter and Newton Abbot

Period	Number of arrivals at Newton Abbot		Average number of minutes lost from Exeter
	Scheduled	Actual	
10.0 - 11.0 am	5	4	18
11.0 - 12.0	9	3	16
12.0 - 1.0 pm	9	7	34
1.0 - 2.0	7	4	44
2.0 - 3.0	9	5	40
3.0 - 4.0	6	8	47
4.0 - 5.0	6	8	46
5.0 - 6.0	7	8	34
6.0 - 7.0	2	8	15
7.0 - 8.0	3	4	27
8.0 - 9.0	2	5	34

Up Trains

There was a greater concentration of up traffic than down traffic on 1957 summer Saturdays, with relatively few overnight services: there were only nine overnight departures from Devon and Cornwall. By day, however, during the six busiest hours from 9.0 to 3.0, 42 regular trains were scheduled to pass Whiteball in the up direction, compared with 38 during the six busiest hours in the down direction. Saturday 27 July 1957 was, however, the peak day for travel to the holiday resorts, and the actual number of down trains exceeded up trains even during the daylight hours; for returning holidaymakers, until the evening, only two extra trains were scheduled, and one of the two 'Q' trains was running. The extras were the 7.15 Paignton-Paddington (which in fact ran every

Saturday thereafter for six weeks) and the 8.30 Paignton-Derby.
63 trains were scheduled to leave for Newton Abbot between 7.0
7.0am and 5.0pm, an average of one every 9½ minutes.

The main Cornish group started with the 7.50 Newquay-Manchester reaching Newton Abbot at 11.0.

Because they were nearer the start of their journeys, it was
normally easier to keep up trains in their correct sequence through
the Newton Abbot-Taunton section. The main operating difficulty
for up trains was the delay to departures from the Torquay branch
caused by the late arrival of their locomotives and stock on overnight trains. This and the consequent out-of-course running was the
chief cause of delay on 27 July. East of Exeter is a 20 mile climb
to Whiteball mostly at 1 in 114/219, and further delays occurred
on this stretch of line.

The first train observed at Dawlish was the 6.35 Paignton, formed
for Blackburn and Batley, and headed by 7310. This train left
Dawlish 40 minutes late, and it is safe to assume there was a delay
in departure caused by the late arrival of the locomotive or stock
at Paignton, although details of the inward working are not known.
By the time this train was next observed approaching Bristol it had
fallen to 91 minutes late. The 6.35 was the first train of the day to
traverse the Newton Abbot-Bristol section, and so it could hardly
have been delayed by a build-up of traffic. The load was not recorded, but 7310 may have lost time climbing from Exeter to
Whiteball or, alternatively, have been delayed by the 8.15 Exeter-
Taunton local. During the next hour some of the trains from the
Torquay branch were nearer to time when seen at Dawlish, but all
lost 20-40 minutes to the Bristol area. The worst was the 7.0 Paignton, 52 minutes late at Dawlish and running behind two trains which
it should have preceded. The train engine, 6363, carried the reporting number, which suggests that 6846 *Ruckley Grange* may have
been added as pilot at the last minute. The 7.0 was a 'Q' train in the
timetable with a pathway as far as Bristol for the LMR line. On this
date its reporting number denoted the North-to-West route and it
was formed for Preston, no doubt for the end of the East Lancs
Wakes Week. In common with other trains at this period it maintained time to Exeter but lost 43 minutes on to Parson Street.

The Paddington trains also lost a lot of time beyond Exeter.
They were probably delayed over Whiteball; then by the time they

reached the Westbury area they were out of course and thus subject to further delays on the section to Reading. When seen at Theale, the 7.15 Paignton was hard on the heels of the 9.27 Westbury-Reading stopping train; the 7.0 Plymouth and 8.0 Kingswear were right behind the 9.0 Weymouth-Paddington semi-fast with 4933 *Himley Hall* on 10 coaches. The regular return working of the 8.0 Kingswear was the 6.30 Paddington-Plymouth via Bristol; but on this date the 6.30 was hauled by 6022 *King Edward III* off the 7.0 Plymouth.

The first two trains whose loads were recorded were the 7.45 Paignton-Newcastle with 6876 *Kingsland Grange* on 13, and the 8.0 Paignton-Huncoat with 5360 on 12. This tends to bear out the theory that early delays to Bristol were caused by overloaded trains climbing from Exeter to Whiteball. (Later in the day another 2-6-0 on 12 coaches took 50 minutes from Exeter to Wellington.) Throughout the morning trains were leaving Newton Abbot out of course; the worst delays were to those originating at Torquay or Paignton rather than those from Kingswear. The 7.25 Plymouth-Paddington, hauled by 4707, reached Newton Abbot one minute early, but was held there 22 minutes to allow the 8.0 Kingswear, running late, to overtake as booked.

Starting with the 8.30 relief to Derby, it seems that Paignton must have used a spare engine, and then sent off the next five departures with the engine destined for the train before, in order to lessen the effect of the late arrivals of engines on down trains. The 8.30, 8.40, 8.52 and 9.5 Paignton all came up without reporting numbers. The 9.43 Paignton-Birmingham (Moor Street) was worked by 6962 *Soughton Hall*, which had gone down tender first on the 8.50 pm Bradford, carrying the reporting number of the 9.5 Paignton. 4983 *Albert Hall* went down carrying the 9.43 Paignton's reporting number, but reappeared on the 10.10. The sequence came to an end when the engine for the 10.10 Paignton-Cardiff, 6904 *Charfield Hall*, which worked down on the 10.10 pm Hull-Paignton, returned to Newton Abbot light engine at 12.42. The reason for this may be that 6904 had worked down with a scratch crew, which would explain the delay to the Hull train at Newton Abbot; otherwise one might have expected *Charfield Hall* to be used on the 10.35 Paignton-Wolverhampton. On the other hand, by the time the 10.10 Hull eventually left Newton Abbot, the rostered engine for the 10.35 Paignton, 6863 *Dolhywel Grange,* was backing on to the 9.5 pm Newcastle-Paignton as booked, and there was little to be gained by using a different engine on the 10.35. The next Paignton departure, the 10.58 to Nottingham, was hauled by 6811 *Cranbourne Grange,* which must have travelled down the branch much earlier as it had not been seen at Newton Abbot that day.

The *Mayflower* ran ahead of the 8.40 Paignton-Nottingham and 8.52 Paignton-Leeds, both of which it should have followed. The table shows the running of these trains on three consecutive Saturdays:

Minutes late at Exeter

	27.7.57	3.8.57	10.8.57
8.40 Paignton	24	32	28
8.52 Paignton	23	35	30

But these two notorious late-runners were the first trains of the day to keep time over the next section, and had actually regained a minute or two each when next observed at Worle Junction and Uphill Junction respectively. This however was at the expense of the 8.30 Paignton-Derby, which had somehow allowed itself to be overtaken between Exeter and Uphill Junction, although it should have run non-stop from Newton Abbot to Bristol.

Good timekeeping on the Exeter-Taunton section did not last long. There was a long gap between the 9.18 Exmouth-Manchester and the *Devonian* when observed east of Taunton, and 7000 *Viscount Portal* was 55 minutes late near Durston. The reason for this delay is completely unknown, unless it was locomotive trouble, but the effect of it lasted a full 2½ hours, during which time there was no let up in the stream of up trains. All trains lost 20-30 minutes between Exeter and Wellington or Taunton right up to the *Torbay Express* which passed Exeter after 1.0 and took just over an hour to pass Wellington. After this there was a sufficient lull in traffic to despatch the 12.45 Exeter-Taunton local, some 20 minutes late.

According to the SR public timetable the 9.18 Exmouth terminated at Exeter Central; the WR advertised it as a through train to Manchester from Exeter St David's. The 'Hall' normally took over from an SR tank engine at Exeter Central.

Meanwhile the Cornish trains and some of the trains from the Torquay branch were reaching Newton Abbot reasonably punctually, and were despatched from there as far as possible in their correct sequence. Thus the 9.5 Kingswear-Swansea was held outside for 5 minutes while the 6.0 Penzance-Manchester changed engines; the 6.0 itself trailed the slower 9.5 Paignton-Manchester and was kept behind it at Exeter. The 7.40 St Austell-Wolverhampton waited 13 minutes at Newton Abbot for the 9.45 Churston-Paddington, with a 202 mile non-stop run from Paignton, to overtake. 5053 *Earl Cairns* on the 13-coach Churston seems to have caught up the 10.15 Teignmouth-Bradford shortly after Dawlish, and, despite stops by the Bradford at Exeter, Tiverton Junction and Taunton, remained behind it all the way to Cogload, where the two diverged. The Churston lost 37 minutes between Dawlish and Taunton but only 9 more minutes over the next 100 miles to Theale.

The 7.50 Newquay-Manchester was the first of three 15-coach trains noted during the day. Its pilot engine, in this case 4970 *Sketty Hall,* normally worked through to Pontypool Road.

The 8.15 Perranporth-Paddington often reached Newton Abbot early (no less than 13 minutes on 10 August 1957). Double-chimney 5043 *Earl of Mount Edgcumbe* was still punctual through Exeter but time was lost on to Taunton in common with all other trains at this period. However, the Perranporth and the two following Paddington trains all gained time between Taunton and Theale. The Perranporth may even have lost some time between Newbury and Reading; when seen at Theale it was only 11 minutes behind a procession consisting of a stopping steam train, an up Weymouth express, a stopping diesel railcar and a light engine.

The 10.35 non-stop Torquay-Paddington passed Newton Abbot 74 minutes late, the worst of the day so far. The engine for this train normally worked down at 9.40 from Newton Abbot to Torre, where it collected the empty coaches and left for Torquay at 10.20. This arrangement was altered on 27 July, and the train was scheduled to come up empty from Paignton leaving at 10.15. But the engine, 5049 *Earl of Plymouth,* did not leave Newton Abbot, running light, until 10.12; it followed 6863 *Dolhywel Grange* on the 9.5 pm Newcastle-Paignton, also running tender first and booked to return on the 10.35 Paignton-Wolverhampton. Unless 5049 was waiting for a crew to arrive, it seems that either the special arrangement had been cancelled or the locomotive department had overlooked it; otherwise there seems no reason why the 'Castle' should not have been attached to an earlier down train, and so saved a valuable block section on this grossly congested line. If it arrived at Torre and found no stock waiting, this would certainly account for its 74 minute late passage through Newton Abbot.

The 10.35 Torquay had a good run to Exeter, trains being fairly well spaced on this section, but lost approximately 27 minutes on to Taunton. The following 10.35 Paignton-Wolverhampton, which made similar progress to Taunton, had reached Newton Abbot 71 minutes late, its locomotive not having left there for Paignton until 10.2.

The next train past Newton Abbot was the 11.30 Torquay, again non-stop to Paddington. The engine and stock for this train worked down from Newton Abbot at 10.50, and was seen to leave on time (see down section). It was due to stop in the up platform at Torquay at 11.10, and the engine to run round, but because of the late running of the 10.35 Torquay and 10.35 Paignton the empty stock must have been held outside Torquay for over half an hour. 6865 *Hopton Grange* was evidently in trouble after Poole Siding, as the 11.30 Torquay was next seen at Savernake behind 6851 *Hurst Grange* of 85A, and having been overtaken by the *Torbay Express.* Engines had probably been changed at either Taunton or Westbury. The 11.30 had lost 21 minutes between Poole Siding and Theale but regained 8 of these to Paddington.

The engine for the *Torbay Express* regularly worked down on the 8.0 Exeter-Kingswear stopping train; although this train was 36 minutes late at Newton Abbot, there should still have been enough time for turnround at Kingswear, and the lateness of the *Torbay* was more likely caused by the previous three trains off the branch. It followed the 11.30 Torquay closely until it was able to get ahead.

The mid-day stopping train from Exeter to Taunton departed in its correct sequence in the procession of up trains, some 20 minutes late. It was booked to stand at Tiverton Junction for 42 minutes to let six more expresses pass and then follow the 10.0 Newquay-Paddington, but because of the out-of-course running the gap between the Newquay and the *Limited* was filled by two Paignton trains; the local's time at Wellington was not recorded, except that it was 'about 2½ hours late', and that 100 passengers who had been waiting 'all afternoon' gave the driver a big cheer. Calculating from the nearest gap in the procession of up expresses passing Wellington, it probably called there about 4.0, a little under two hours late.

Throughout the morning trains had been covering the Newton Abbot-Exeter section with little loss of time, until 6913 *Levens Hall* on the 14-coach 12.18 Newton Abbot-Paddington. This train departed in its correct order at 12.33 and, with stops at Teignmouth and Dawlish, took all but an hour to reach Exeter, a loss of approximately 19 minutes. It was probably the frequent stops with a heavy train that caused 6913 to lose time, because from Exeter onwards it kept up with the 11.15 Plymouth which had overtaken it; but its running as far as Exeter had serious repercussions on all up trains for the next hour. The seven following trains, including the *Limited*, lost an average of 19 minutes between Newton Abbot and Exeter. The 12.18's progress resulted in a lull in traffic on the section east of Exeter, and losses between Exeter and Wellington for the next half-hour were of the order of only 7-14 minutes. The observer at Wellington commented on the high speed of all up trains passing that point.

The 11.15 Plymouth-Paddington may have been slightly delayed in departure awaiting its pilot engine, 6856 *Stowe Grange.* This engine had worked into Plymouth as pilot on the 11.35 pm Liverpool-Penzance, which had not left Newton Abbot until 10.6. At Brent the 11.15 attached a portion from Kingsbridge. By overtaking the 12.18 Newton Abbot at Exeter as scheduled it got a clear run, but by Wellington it had caught up the *Torbay Express* which was at the tail end of the previous group of trains.

From then on, however, the 11.15 Plymouth lost time very badly indeed, on track with far less density of traffic. 55 minutes were lost between Wellington and Theale, and the 11.30 Torquay, which must have passed Wellington some 15 minutes ahead of the Plymouth, was 32 minutes ahead at Theale even after an unscheduled engine change. A possible explanation for part of this loss is that the Plymouth was unlucky enough to get behind a stopping train on the Taunton to Castle Cary section. The 2.30 Taunton-Castle Cary via Durston was scheduled to call at Athelney at 2.49, after the passing of the up *Limited.* The group of Paddington trains ending with the *Limited* were running about 40 minutes late, but the local was unlikely to have been held at Taunton for this length of time as it would have had a clear road via the Durston loop. Thus the local train may have regained the main line at Athelney just ahead of the 11.15 Plymouth; with a schedule of 41 minutes to Castle Cary it could have caused the express to drop up to 20 minutes here. Whatever the cause of the rest of the delay to the 11.15 Plymouth, three following trains were severely delayed in turn. Four up expresses passed Theale in the space of 23 minutes, having lost between 43 and 55 minutes from Wellington. The other stopping train in the area at this time, the 2.20 Bristol-Reading, must have been held at Patney & Chirton for the whole of this procession, since it did not reach Savernake until after the *Limited*.

The 12.5 Paignton-Cardiff was 27 minutes late at Newton Abbot, and may have been the indirect cause of delay to the 8.20 Penzance-Paddington. It may have been intended to allow the Cardiff to precede the 8.20 to Exeter as booked, but that 5341 took longer than expected on the climb out of Torquay and then seemed intent on taking the full station allowance of 8 minutes (+1) at Newton Abbot. By this time, with the 9.20 St Ives-Paddington waiting to enter, it may have been decided to allow the two Cornish expresses to go first. The lateness of the 12.5 Paignton could hardly have been due to the late arrival of its engine, which had left Newton Abbot in plenty of time on the 6.5 Cardiff. On the other hand the 12.5 may have been the one Paignton departure affected by late arrival of stock as opposed to engine. The stock was due down on the 12.8 am Manchester, which (if correctly identified) must have reached Paignton about 1.0 pm; in this case fresh stock must have been provided at short notice for the 12.5.

The 8.20 Penzance-Paddington spent 14 minutes at Newton Abbot. The 9.20 St Ives-Paddington was close behind, but did not overtake at Exeter as booked. Thus the St Ives lost 37 minutes between Newton Abbot and Wellington compared with 15 minutes by the 8.20 Penzance. The 8.20 was presumably overtaken at Taunton.

The next in the group of London-bound expresses was 6000 *King George V* on the 10.0 from Newquay. This was a regular 15-coach load and carried passengers from Newquay and St Columb Road for Paddington only. Between Newton Abbot and Wellington *King George V* lost time uniformly with the group, but went on to lose a total of no less than 63 minutes between Wellington and Theale. The reason for this was that, besides forming part of the procession headed by the 11.15 Plymouth, the Newquay when observed at Theale was being checked by the 4.20 Hungerford-Reading stopping train running 30 minutes late. The Newquay was probably close behind the 8.20 Penzance until the local was despatched from Newbury between them; the *Limited*, following closely, was also suffering checks at Theale.

The 12.5 Paignton, leaving Newton Abbot 28 minutes late, was no less than 68 minutes late at Wellington. It was delayed as far as Exeter by the cumulative effect of the 12.18 Newton Abbot's running. Leaving Exeter only 2 minutes after the 10.0 Newquay passed through, and with its 12-coach load, 5341 took 50 minutes for the 23½ miles from Exeter to Wellington, causing another series of delays on this section, so that the next three trains, including the *Limited*, lost an average of 24 minutes. Then came a lull in departures from Exeter.

After the *Limited* there was a gap of 29 minutes at Newton Abbot before the departure of the 10.5 Penzance-Liverpool, and so the next three trains kept time as far as Exeter. The 10.5 then caught up the procession in front, but the following 11.0 Newquay-York stopped at Exeter and did not leave there until 25 minutes after the 10.5 had passed. 4075 *Cardiff Castle* on 14 coaches was only 7 minutes behind the 10.5 at Wellington, having dropped 6 minutes.

The 10.20 Penzance-Swansea was booked non-stop from Plymouth to Exeter, where it detached its pilot. The two 'Granges' took only 49 minutes to pass Newton Abbot after hauling their 13-coach load for 32 miles including Hemerdon and Dainton banks. With a clear road east the 10.20 was only 5 minutes late at Wellington. 6860 *Aberporth Grange* returned to Plymouth as pilot on the 12.5 Paddington.

The next train at Newton Abbot was the 12.15 Kingswear-Wolverhampton which arrived there 55 minutes late. The reason for this is not known. The engine, 4037 *The South Wales Borderers,* had not previously been recorded that day. The stock should have presented no problem: its formation was 6 from Kingswear, the regular *Cornishman* set, a van added at Churston, and 6 from Paignton which should have been stabled since the Saturday before. The 12.15 was allowed 12 minutes at Newton Abbot for the up *Limited* to overtake: the *Limited* having passed 45 minutes earlier, 4 minutes were regained here. Then the 12.15 took all but an hour to reach Exeter, with four intermediate stops, a loss of approximately 13 minutes no doubt caused partly by the heavy load and partly by overcrowding at stations. Such slow progress by a train running out of course caused the utmost delay to the trains following, all of which had faster timings over the section. The repercussions were felt for an hour, and the next seven trains lost an average of 29 minutes between Newton Abbot and Exeter.

Immediately behind the 12.15 was 5959 *Mawley Hall* and 14 coaches on the 1.30 Paignton-Paddington non-stop. The 1.30 was already late as its engine had worked down from Newton Abbot, as booked, on the 7.40 Paddington, which did not leave there until 12.37. The stock was also booked in on the 7.40 Paddington, but a substitute set was presumably found (the 7.40 had only 11 coaches). The 1.30 Paignton stopped at Exeter from 3.23 to 3.27; although the reason is not known for certain, it was probably to take water. This was not an uncommon procedure, in the event of a train being heavily delayed between Newton Abbot and Exeter and unable to pick up sufficient water at Exminster troughs. Half an hour later the up *Cornishman* made a 6 minute unscheduled stop at Exeter which was probably for the same reason.

While the 1.30 Paignton was at Exeter the 11.15 Waterloo-Plymouth, Padstow and Bude was evidently given precedence; the departure of the Southern train was recorded at 3.26, and it would have been in front of the Paignton as far as Cowley Bridge Junction. Also in the station was the 12.15 Kingswear-Wolverhampton, pre-sumably in platform 6: the 1.30 Paignton did succeed in overtaking this train, as booked, but then lost 14 minutes on to Wellington. This may have been due to the heavy load, but it seems more likely that the 12.45 Exeter-Taunton was allowed to leave Tiverton Junction in the gap which followed the 10.20 Penzance-Swansea, and that the 1.30 had caught up with the local.

The 11.15 Newquay-Wolverhampton, after losing 36 minutes on the 20 miles from Newton Abbot to Exeter, also overtook the 12.15 Kingswear and so lost only 7 more minutes on to Wellington. The 12.15, departing from Exeter almost simultaneously, lost 15 min-utes on to Wellington, thus causing another, though less serious, chain of delays on that section, so that the nine following trains lost an average of 16 minutes between Exeter and Wellington. The

1.55 Torquay-Paddington and 1.55 Paignton-Wolverhampton, both with fairly fast timings, were caught in both series of delays, and so lost 48 and 51 minutes respectively between Newton Abbot and Wellington. The 1.55 Torquay was scheduled to depart empty from Paignton at 1.40, using the stock of the 8.10 Newport. The engine also went down on the 8.10 Newport, as booked, and so did not leave Newton Abbot for Paignton until 1.18. The 1.55 Paignton-Wolverhampton was supposed to be formed of the stock of the 6.5 Cardiff, which would not have presented any problems, but its engine was booked down on the branch portion of the 7.0 Birmingham. This train did not reach Newton Abbot until 1.44, and 5939 *Tangley Hall,* the engine in question, was sent down light at 1.37; the branch portion of the 7.0 Birmingham was eventually terminated at Newton Abbot.

The packed 10.45 Penzance-Sheffield and the 11.10 Penzance-Wolverhampton were both delayed between Newton Abbot and Exeter by the reaction from the 12.15 Kingswear. The 11.10, despite its 6 minute stop at Exeter, overtook the 10.45 as scheduled: although leaving Exeter 19 minutes after the previous train, the 11.10 had caught up with the stream of traffic ahead by Wellington.

The 1.40 Kingswear-Paddington was 37 minutes late at Newton Abbot. It was the return working for the engine and stock of the 7.5 Paddington; thus 6957 *Norcliffe Hall,* which had worked into Newton Abbot on the 10.10 pm Hull-Paignton, did not leave there for Kingswear until 12.20. The 1.40 Kingswear stopped at Teignmouth and Dawlish, and was overtaken at Exeter by two Cornish trains which had left Newton Abbot 36 and 45 minutes behind it. These two, the 12.30 Newquay-Paddington and the *Royal Duchy,* should have had a fairly clear run to Exeter, but the Newquay inexplicably lost 11 minutes between Newton Abbot and Dawlish. After Exeter they caught up with the procession ahead, but lost less time to Wellington than most trains at this period. The 12.30 Newquay was the first Cornish train to be substantially delayed west of Newton Abbot, but lost only 13 minutes overall between Plymouth and Wellington, the area covered by observers at this time.

The 2.25 Paignton-Sheffield and 2.45 Paignton-Paddington were 71 and 64 minutes late at Newton Abbot. The engines for both these trains worked down from Newton Abbot to Paignton on the

8.10 Paddington, and must have reached Paignton some time after 3.0. This was the booked working for the 2.25, but the 2.45 engine should have worked the 8.50 Paddington from Newton Abbot. However, if 5067 *St Fagan's Castle* had kept to its booked working it would not have left Newton Abbot for Paignton until 4.12. The 2.25 was formed from the stock of the 9.5 pm Newcastle-Paignton, and was headed by 5027 *Farleigh Castle,* which had brought this same stock into Newton Abbot at 9.47 am. Both trains had a clear run to Exeter but were delayed further east by the build up following the slow running of the 12.15 Kingswear-Wolverhampton. The 2.25 passed Exeter only 6 minutes after the departure of the 1.40 Kingswear-Paddington, and must have been delayed severely almost at once; yet *Farleigh Castle* was 12 minutes behind the 1.40 passing Wellington.

The 12.50 Newquay-Cardiff, a 10-coach load, was one of the few expresses scheduled to be worked over the South Devon banks by a single engine. However, 7013 *Bristol Castle* was prevented from making its non-stop run through Newton Abbot, as it reached there at the same time as the 2.45 Paignton-Paddington, and was stopped by signals on the through line for 2 minutes.

The 4.5 Exeter to Weston-Super-Mare stopping train departed 43 minutes late and virtually kept time to Taunton. It had a scheduled wait of 17 minutes at Cullompton for two expresses to overtake. This appears to have taken place, but the two trains which overtook were not the two specified in the working timetable. The first was the 12.50 Newquay, not booked to pass the local until Taunton; the 12.50 dropped 10 minutes between Exeter and Wellington, which may have been caused by the stopping train in front.

The 2.55 and 3.10 Paignton-Wolverhampton were unusual in 1957 in that they began their journeys with the engines off the 7.30 Birmingham (Moor Street) and 6.55 Wolverhampton, which worked tender first from Paignton and were replaced at Newton Abbot. On 27 July the workings seem to have been altered slightly as the engines concerned were those off the 6.30 Wolverhampton relief and 7.30 Birmingham respectively. These two did not leave Newton Abbot until 3.13 and 3.30, and the engines were 80 and 97 minutes late when they re-appeared on the up trains.

The 2.55 had a good run, being 32 minutes behind the previous train at Newton Abbot and 22 at Exeter, and from this time, 5.0

pm onwards, little time was lost between either Newton Abbot and Exeter or Exeter and Wellington/Taunton.

The next train at Newton Abbot was the 3.20 Kingswear-Cardiff, 41 minutes late. This was the return working of the engine, 6915 *Mursley Hall,* and stock of the 8.5 Cardiff-Kingswear, which left Newton Abbot nearly 2½ hours late and must have reached Kingswear about 3.30.

The 15-coach 12.0 Penzance-Manchester spent 30 minutes at Plymouth, leaving there 23 minutes late. The reason for this is unknown: neither engine which took over at Plymouth had been observed previously. At Exeter the Penzance was overtaken by the 3.10 Paignton-Wolverhampton using platform 6, and stopping for only 3 minutes instead of the 11 allowed. The progress of these two trains to Bristol was recorded by observers returning from Wellington and Dawlish respectively. The 3.10 Paignton had an unchecked run from Exeter until just before Bristol, and drew into Temple Meads simultaneously with the 12.0 Penzance. The Penzance was completely unchecked from Taunton to Bristol, and 6916 *Misterton Hall* kept up a speed in the 50s from Cogload to Parson Street with a maximum of 62 mph.

The 1.45 Newquay-Paddington reached Plymouth 38 minutes late and was taken over by 1000 *County of Middlesex* which had arrived on the 5.30 pm Glasgow and should have returned east on the 11.0 Newquay-York. The 1.45 Newquay gained time as far as Newton Abbot but was checked beyond, as it left Newton Abbot only 5 minutes behind the 3.10 Paignton-Wolverhampton calling at Teignmouth and Dawlish. The Newquay must also have been checked at Exeter, as the other platform was occupied by the 12.0 Penzance, but the effect of all this was lightened by the Newquay's allowance of 9 minutes recovery time between Newton Abbot and Exeter. It is not certain whether the Newquay or the Penzance got the road out of Exeter first, but no time was being lost on the Exeter-Taunton section at this hour, and the Newquay was still only 45 minutes late passing Taunton. The following 1.20 Penzance-Paddington was similarly late at Plymouth and also lost time between Newton Abbot and Exeter.

The 14-coach 4.15 Paignton-Paddington, which reached Newton Abbot 73 minutes late, was the return working of the stock of the 8.50 Paddington, which did not leave Newton Abbot until 4.12. Its locomotives, 5934 *Kneller Hall* and 6904 *Charfield Hall,* had also worked down from Newton Abbot on the 8.50 Paddington, although this was not the scheduled working; this train was often double-headed in the early part of the season, the engines normally running light from Newton Abbot to Paignton. The 4.15 was not booked to call at Newton Abbot, but in fact stopped there for 8 minutes; it appears to have been checked by the 12.20 Penzance-Kensington milk, and overtaken the milk train at Dawlish Warren.

The 4.40 Paignton-Bristol stopping train was the only up passenger train hauled by an engine which had evidently used the new Goodrington turntable. It was booked to be worked throughout by the Bath Road engine off the 7.30 Paddington-Kingswear, but this train did not leave Newton Abbot until 4.14. The 4.40 instead began its journey with 5991 *Gresham Hall* off the 6.55 Wolverhampton, which must have had very little turn-round time since its arrival at Paignton; despite having been turned, it was replaced at Newton Abbot by 6391 off the 5.20 Coventry-Paignton relief. Whether because of the non-arrival of its booked locomotive, or because it was held back at Paignton until the 4.15 to Paddington had departed, the 4.40 was 59 minutes late at Newton Abbot.

7901 *Dodington Hall,* having arrived at Kingswear on the 7.30 Paddington, was used on the 5.30 stopping train to Taunton, and the two remaining departures observed from Kingswear, both local trains, were headed by engines that should have worked the previous train, following the pattern of several of the morning departures from Paignton. The engines concerned were 5981 *Frensham Hall* and 6874 *Haughton Grange.*

Between 6.30 and 7.30 pm all up trains were severely delayed in the Newton Abbot area because of the clear road given to a Millbay-Paddington Ocean Liner Express which passed at 6.59. The 5.15 Paignton-Nottingham arrived at Newton Abbot 50 minutes late at 6.28 with its rostered engine, 6997 *Bryn-Ivor Hall,* which had worked the 6.40 Leicester from Bristol. 6997 must have reached Paignton by 5.0, but needed a longer turn-round time before working back to Bristol again, and so worked to Newton Abbot tender first to be replaced there by 6819 *Highnam Grange.* The 'Grange' had arrived at Paignton on the 7.20 Birmingham (New Street) relief, and returned light to Newton Abbot at 3.27. Meanwhile the 2.35 Penzance-Glasgow relief departed ahead of the 5.15

Paignton. This train had not been observed for certain at Plymouth, but is thought to have left there about 5.35, its pilot, 70024 *Vulcan,* having arrived there at 5.10 on the 9.30 Paddington-Newquay; it was booked non-stop between Plymouth and Exeter, but in fact stopped at Newton Abbot to detach the pilot, and must also have been sidetracked at Dawlish Warren for the boat train. The 2.35 reached Exeter at approximately 7.35, 44 minutes late. The 5.15 Paignton-Nottingham was held at Newton Abbot for the boat train, and so left there 77 minutes late after a stop of 32 minutes.

The 4.35 Kingswear-Paddington was the return working of the engine (as far as Newton Abbot only) and stock of the 10.20 Paddington, which must have reached Kingswear about 5.30. The 4.35 may also have been delayed entering Newton Abbot by the fact that there was no available platform there until 6.42; it eventually arrived 84 minutes late and was held 11 minutes over time because of the boat train. Not surprisingly, approximately 10 minutes were lost on to Exeter, being the third departure from Newton Abbot in the space of five minutes.

The three trains arriving at Newton Abbot between 7.0 and 7.30 were between 30 and 70 minutes late, some of which was no doubt due to the platforms being occupied by trains waiting for the up Millbay to pass. The first was the 5.30 Paignton-Paddington relief, the booked return working of the engine and stock of the 10.40 Paddington-Paignton; this train was originally scheduled to run empty to Didcot, but altered at the last minute to a passenger train. It was delayed firstly by the late arrival of the 10.40, then probably by the congestion at Newton Abbot, and finally lost about 15 minutes between Newton Abbot and Exeter by being the fourth departure from Newton Abbot in 10 minutes.

The 5.30 Kingswear-Taunton stopping train, running 50 minutes late after awaiting the arrival of its engine, had a scheduled wait of 38 minutes at Exeter, and so was able to cut its lateness by over half an hour.

The 1.55 Penzance-Newton Abbot stopping train was on time at Plymouth, but lost 33 minutes on the final section of its journey. This train must have been shunted at some stage to allow the Millbay boat train to pass, and was probably also delayed at the approaches to Newton Abbot by the 5.30 Kingswear, which had been crossed to the up main line at Aller Junction to overtake an empty train from Paignton headed by 7811 *Dunley Manor* running tender first.

The 6.7 Plymouth-Bristol was booked to be worked as far as Newton Abbot by the engine off the 8.17 Carmarthen-Penzance, and from Newton Abbot onwards by the engine off the 8.45 Liverpool-Penzance. The Carmarthen was due at Plymouth at 4.45 but was last seen approaching there 2 hours 10 minutes late. 5023 *Brecon Castle,* which had worked in on the 1.45 Newquay, was put on the 6.7, and got away 29 minutes late. At Newton Abbot there was a further hour's delay awaiting 4963 *Rignall Hall* on the 8.45 Liverpool. This engine, which presumably worked from Shrewsbury, was due at 4.50, allowing three hours for turn-round. On this occasion it arrived at 7.49 and took one hour to turn round; thus the 6.7 Plymouth left Newton Abbot 94 minutes late after a wait of 71 minutes. The 8.17 Carmarthen engine, 5005 *Manorbier Castle,* in fact worked back on the 4.20 Penzance-Newton Abbot, due to leave Plymouth at 7.10. The 8.17 must have reached Plymouth about 6.55, and the 4.20 terminated at Newton Abbot 30 minutes late at 8.53. Part of this delay may have been due to awaiting a platform at Newton Abbot, as the 6.7 Plymouth did not depart until 8.48, and a stopping train from the branch terminated at 8.43. Local branch trains were not adhering to their booked engine workings during this period and are difficult to identify. Seven were due to call at Newton Abbot between 6.30 and 9.30 pm, mostly formed from the stock of down expresses. The train at 8.43 was headed by the engine off the 10.35 Wolverhampton, and may have been a combination of the 6.30 Goodrington and 7.15 Paignton.

Meanwhile the 6.30 Kingswear arrived at Newton Abbot 47 minutes late and changed engines as scheduled, 5981 *Frensham Hall* working forward on the 7.50 parcels to Taunton. The 6.30 waited 27 minutes at Newton Abbot before 5150, which had been on shed all day, took it on to Exeter.

Other Lines

It is difficult to assess the effect of the West of England chaos on other parts of the Region, as few records have come to light. Observations at Paddington for an hour in the morning and an hour in the afternoon do not suggest that the delays spread to other parts. The 11.55 Paddington-Pembroke Dock is known to have departed Cardiff 109 minutes late. At Paddington the 3.55 am and the 4.25 am Fishguard Harbour terminated early, while the 6.15 am Swansea and the *Capitals United Express* were 10 and 23 minutes late. In the afternoon the 10.20 Pembroke Dock and 11.10 Milford Haven both arrived about 20 minutes late.

A relief to the 7.0 Weston-super-Mare arrived at Paddington from Bristol 33 minutes late and behind the main train. The only other Bristol line train observed at Paddington was 5035 *Coity Castle* on the 1.58 Weston-super-Mare (Locking Road), which terminated 3 minutes early; this train probably escaped delay in the Bristol area because it departed during a period of low intensity on the Taunton-Bristol section, when the main group of trains for Paddington were passing Taunton.

A very full record of observations throughout the day at Southampton Central throws some light on what conditions may have been on the WR. Early Bristol-Portsmouth trains were punctual at Southampton until the 9.0 Cardiff, 10.50 Bristol, 10.8 Cardiff which were uniformly just over 20 minutes late. The position then and 10.30 Cardiff which were uniformly just over 20 minutes late. The position then deteriorated with the 12.53 Cardiff-Portsmouth arriving 40 minutes late and the 1.0 Cardiff-Brighton 64 minutes late. These delays may of course have been unconnected with the WR; although numerous West of England trains, particularly up trains, must have been out of course at Bristol, there may not have been such congestion there as to delay trains travelling in other directions.

Other trains, destined for Bournemouth, reached Southampton via Oxford and Basingstoke. These trains were within 15 minutes of time until the 9.30 Birkenhead, 10.17 York relief, 10.15 Bradford and 12.10 Sheffield, which were between 24 and 50 minutes late. The delays were no doubt caused in part by the Southampton tunnel bottleneck, aggravated on this afternoon by a short-lived signal failure. Last to arrive was the 8.37 Newcastle, headed by 30781 *Sir Aglovale,* 94 minutes late and out of course behind the Sheffield. The Newcastle traversed WR metals from Banbury Junction to Southcote Junction, Reading, perhaps too remote from the area of delay in Devon and Somerset.

Locomotives

Summary of locomotives recorded on express passenger duty, including pilots, in the West of England area of the WR on 27 July 1957:

KING	12	GRANGE	26
CASTLE	42	MANOR	7
STAR	1	43XX	10
COUNTY	9	47XX	2
HALL	51	41XX	7
Modified HALL	13	BRITANNIA	1

There appears to have been no shortage of 'Kings' on the West of England line; they were generally confined to Paddington trains, and all those usually 'King'-hauled on a peak summer Saturday were so hauled. The majority of West of England holiday expresses in the 1950s were handled by the 'Castle', 'County', 'Hall', Modified 'Hall' and 'Grange' classes. The only remaining 'Star', 4056 *Princess Margaret,* worked the 9.15 Liverpool-Plymouth as far as Newton Abbot.

Only one BR standard type was seen in the West of England, 'Britannia' 70024 *Vulcan,* which arrived at Newton Abbot on the 6.35 Walsall-Kingswear and later worked as a pilot engine to Plymouth and back. Several 'Manors' were at work west of Newton Abbot, mainly as pilots over the South Devon banks; the only one noted east of Newton Abbot was 7811 *Dunley Manor,* which hauled the 10.37 Cardiff-Paignton relief.

43XX Class 2-6-0s were used on three early morning departures from Paignton: 7310 on the 6.35 to Blackburn and Batley; 6363, piloted by 6846 *Ruckley Grange,* on the 7.0 to Preston; and 5360 on the 8.0 Paignton-Huncoat. 5341 was on the 12.5 departure for Cardiff. Two more worked into Paignton during the day, 6391 on the 5.20 Coventry relief, and 5385 on the 9.25 Wolverhampton.

The two 47XX 2-8-0s observed were 4707 on the 7.25 Plymouth-Paddington and 4704 on the 8.25 Ilfracombe-Manchester. No 28XX 2-8-0s were seen on passenger duties.

Two Penzance (83G) engines were seen east of Newton Abbot: 1002 *County of Berks* on the 11.35 pm Liverpool-Penzance; and

6824 *Ashley Grange* on the 7.0 Swindon-Penzance.

Four engines from Shrewsbury (84G) were observed: 1016 *County of Hants* on the 6.0 Penzance-Liverpool; 1025 *County of Radnor* went as far as Plymouth on the 7.0 Birmingham-Penzance; 7811 *Dunley Manor* on the 10.37 Cardiff-Paignton relief; 5968 *Cory Hall* worked a regular turn (subject to the correct identification of the overnight train) on the 12.8 am Manchester-Paignton and the 3.10 Paignton-Wolverhampton, but was removed from the down train at Newton Abbot instead of Paignton.

The four Worcester (85A) engines seen were 6950 *Kingsthorpe Hall* on the Kidderminster-Paignton relief, returning on the empty stock; 6807 *Birchwood Grange* worked to Newton Abbot on the first part of the 6.55 Wolverhampton, originating at West Bromwich; 7013 *Bristol Castle* headed the 12.50 Newquay-Cardiff (which a fortnight later was in the hands of a Chester locomotive); 6851 *Hurst Grange* at some stage replaced another Grange on the 11.30 Torquay-Paddington.

A Hereford (85C) engine, 6916 *Misterton Hall*, worked the 12.0 Penzance-Manchester, and a Gloucester (85B) engine, 5907 *Marble Hall*, having obviously arrived in the area on an overnight relief, was seen on the 6.20 am Paignton-Exminster ECS and later went on shed at Exeter.

Eleven engines from the three principal sheds in the Birmingham area visited the West of England, two from Stafford Road (84A), seven from Oxley (84B) and two from Tyseley (84E). Three of these were working to and from Paddington: 5045 *Earl of Dudley* (84A) on the 8.20 Penzance; 6904 *Charfield Hall* (84E) was one of the engines of the 4.15 Paignton; and 6879 *Overton Grange* (84B) worked the 7.40 Paddington-Paignton and 5.30 Paignton-Paddington. Another Oxley engine, 5341, headed the 12.5 Paignton-Cardiff.

Another London train worked by an engine from a shed well off its route was the 11.30 Torquay-Paddington, which began its journey behind 6865 *Hopton Grange* of Newport (86A).

Conversely, several London Division engines were noted on cross-country trains. Two of these were from Old Oak Common: 6962 *Soughton Hall* on the 9.43 Paignton-Birmingham via Swindon; 7903 *Foremarke Hall* worked the 9.5 Paignton-Manchester, presumably as far as Shrewsbury, and returned on the 3.10 Manchester-Plymouth. A Reading (81D) engine, 4960 *Pyle Hall,* travelled to

Bristol and back on the 8.5 Newquay-Newcastle and 9.25 Bradford-Paignton; 5983 *Henley Hall,* of Southall (81C) shed, having arrived in Plymouth on the 6.55 Paddington, was next seen on the 2.35 Penzance-Glasgow.

LOCOMOTIVE WORKINGS ON THE KINGSWEAR BRANCH 27 JULY 1957

| Engine Number | DOWN | | | | | UP | | | | |
	Code Carried	Train	Time ex NA	Mins late	Destination	Code carried	Train	Time arr NA	Mins late	Notes
6876						533	7.45 Paignton	8.25	18	
5360						578	8.00 Paignton	8.44	17	
6938						505	8.00 Kingswear	8.55	12	
6856						-	LE -	9.00	-	
6814						(546)	8.30 Paignton	9.11	16	
4914						(543)	8.40 Paignton	9.20	19	
4980						(553)	8.52 Paignton	9.32	18	
7000						563	8.45 Kingswear	9.40	1E	
7903						(579)	9.05 Paignton	9.58	27	
5079						580	9.05 Kingswear	10.12	13	
5053						510	9.45 Churston	10.31	8	
6962	R 579	415	8.57	129	Paignton	527	9.43 Paignton	10.40	33	
4983	R 527	258	9.07	112	Paignton	585	10.10 Paignton	10.54	23	
5934						-	LE -	11.05	-	
6954	412	412	9.21	145	Paignton	-	LE -	11.05	-	
6965						588	10.20 Kingswear	11.24	12	
6811						573	10.58 Paignton	11.34	9	
5907							ECS	11.52	-	
5049	R 515	9.40 NA	10.12	32	LE Torre?	515	10.35 Torquay	12.02	74	
6863	R 537	418	10.02	104	Paignton	537	10.35 Paignton	12.09	71	
6865	R 525	10.50 NA	10.50	T	ECS Torquay	525	11.30 Torquay	12.22	40	
5038	-	8.00 EXE	9.31	35	Kingswear	520	11.20 Kingswear	12.31	19	
5986	230	268?	9.42	97	Paignton	-	LE -	12.42	-	

(continued overleaf)

DOWN

Engine Number	Code carried	Train	Time ex NA	Mins late	Destination	Code carried	Train	Time arr NA	Mins late	Notes
6904	R 585	417	9.50	120	Paignton	-	LE	12.42	-	
5341	R 590	700	10.26	22	Paignton	590	12.05 Paignton	12.56	27	
5011	R 594	9.32 NA	9.55	23	Paignton	594	12.30 Paignton	1.08	6	
1024	422	422	8.36	128	Paignton	-	LE	1.15	-	
4176						-	LE	1.15	-	
6950	835	835	11.25	27	Paignton	R -	ECS	1.34	-	
4150	-	230?	12.31	198	Paignton	-	LE	1.47	-	
4037					Kingswear	557	12.15 Kingswear	2.11	55	
5959	R 550	108	12.37	73	Paignton	530	1.30 Paignton	2.28	38	
6391	427	427	12.54	86	Paignton	-	LE	2.34	-	
3677	-	9.30 EXE	11.11	39	Kingswear	-	LE	2.34	-	
5078	R 540	703	1.18	106	Paignton	540	1.55 Torquay	2.43	36	
5939	567	-	1.37	-	LE Paignton	567	1.55 Paignton	2.52	34	
6957	535	103	12.20	66	Kingswear	535	1.40 Kingswear	3.07	37	
4988	096	096	12.41	82	Paignton	-	ECS	3.14	-	Ex 096
6819	428	428	2.23	125	Paignton	-	LE	3.27	-	
5950	106	106	2.03	150	Paignton	-	LE	3.32	-	
5027	R 583	110	2.41	134	Paignton	583	2.25 Paignton	4.00	71	Ex 418
5067	R 545	110	2.41	134	Paignton	545	2.45 Paignton	4.15	64	
5976	814	814	3.13	151	Paignton	R(577)	2.55 Paignton	4.45	80	OFF/6954 ON
6915	704	704	2.31	143	Kingswear	595	3.20 Kingswear	4.59	41	OFF/5968 ON
6872	812	812	3.30	157	Paignton	R(587)	3.10 Paignton	5.12	97	
5934) 6904)	R 550	117	4.12	174	Paignton	550	4.15 Paignton	5.53	73	
5991	815	815	3.46	138	Paignton	(599)	4.40 Paignton	6.04	59	OFF/6391 ON

Engine Number	Code carried	Train	Time ex NA	Mins late	Destination	Code carried	Train	Time arr NA	Mins late	Notes
5933	125	125	4.29	163	Paignton	-	LE	6.10	-	
6997	433	433	4.27	156	Paignton	R(593)	5.15 Paignton	6.28	50	OFF/6819 ON
7910	128	128	4.24	149	Kingswear	(555)	4.35 Kingswear	6.47	84	OFF/7025 ON
6879	R -	135	5.03	158	Paignton	(558)	5.30 Paignton	7.04	71	
7901	107	107	4.14	158	Kingswear	-	5.30 Kingswear	7.14	51	
7811	706	706	4.53	133	Paignton	R -	ECS	7.28	-	
4943	823	823	6.19	150	Paignton	R -	LE	7.30	-	
5385	855	855	5.50	165	Paignton	-	ECS	7.55	-	
5981	705	705	5.15	140	Kingswear	-	6.30 Kingswear	8.09	-	OFF/6856 ON
4955	827	827	6.32	128	Paignton	R -	6.30 Goodrington ?	8.43	47	OFF/5150 ON
5967	439	439	6.57	162	Paignton	-	ECS	9.02	103?	
9462						-	LE	9.08	-	
4098	146	146	5.59	143	Kingswear	-	ECS	9.25	-	
6874	-	438	6.20	145	Kingswear	-	7.20 Kingswear?	9.30	81?	
5178	-	430	3.28	150	Kingswear					
4962	149	149	7.29	114	Kingswear					
4105	-	4.47 NA	7.13	137	Kingswear					
5183	-	5.03 NA	8.08	179	Paignton					
4976	R -	441	8.11	144	Paignton					
5072	212	212	8.21	176	Paignton					
5922	442	444	8.33	148	Paignton					
5195	-	6.25 NA	8.58	155	Kingswear					
6814	444	442	8.47	173	Paignton					
5954	152	152	9.27	135	Kingswear					
4960	446	446	9.33	113	Paignton					
7300	-	7.15 EXE	?	?	Paignton					

KEY

R - Tender first

(558) - Code allocated, but not carried

For other notes see page 141

Locomotives used again after working into Newton Abbot (excluding engines employed solely on pilot duties between Newton Abbot and Plymouth)

FIRST WORKING

Engine	Shed	Train	Time arr. NA
7034	82A	8.45 pm Bradford	8.40
5078	83A	10.30 pm Manchester	8.51
6957	82A	10.10 pm Hull	9.20
5027	82A	9.5 pm Newcastle	9.47
5067	82A	6.5 Cardiff	10.15
5934	83D	LE Ex Paignton	11.5
6954	82A	LE Ex Paignton (10.45 pm Rotherham)	11.5
6913	83D	P 7.30 Penzance-Bristol	11.32
5019	82A	7.0 Paddington	11.56
7025	81A	7.5 Paddington	12.11
5968	84G	12.8 Manchester	12.18
6879	84B	7.40 Paddington	12.25
4931	83G	P 8.20 Penzance-Paddington	12.45
5921	86A	8.10 Newport	12.58
7809		P 9.20 St Ives-Paddington	1.2
7916	83A	8.10 Paddington	2.30
4087	83D	P 11.15 Newquay-Wolverhampton	2.34
6391	82B	LE Ex Paignton (5.20 Coventry)	2.34
4088	83D	P 11.10 Penzance-Wolverhampton	2.58
6874	83B	{ 7.20 Taunton-Exeter { P 6.35 Walsall }	3.18
70024	86C	6.35 Walsall	3.18
6819	86G	LE Ex Paignton (7.20 Birmingham NS)	3.27
1015	83D	P 12.30 Newquay-Paddington	3.41
6026	83D	10.30 Paddington	4.32
4976	83D	P 1.20 Penzance-Paddington	5.33
4963	84B	8.45 Liverpool	7.49

For notes see page 141

| | | NEXT WORKING | Time spent at NA | |
Time ex NA		Train	Hrs	Mins
12.59	P	9.35 Bristol-Penzance	4	19
1.18		8.10 Newport-Paignton	4	27
12.20		7.5 Paddington-Kingswear	3	0
2.41		8.10 Paddington-Paignton	4	54
2.41		8.10 Paddington-Paignton	4	26
4.12		8.50 Paddington-Paignton	5	7
4.52		2.55 Paignton-Wolverhampton	5	47
12.33		12.18 NA-Paddington	1	1
3.52	P	7.25 Ealing-Penzance	3	56
7.4		4.35 Kingswear-Paddington	6	53
5.24		3.10 Paignton-Wolverhampton	5	6
5.3		10.40 Paddington-Paignton	4	38
4.37	P	10.30 Paddington-St Ives	3	52
5.54	P	8.55 Wolverhampton-Penzance	4	56
4.37		10.30 Paddington-St Ives	3	35
5.25	P	8.17 Carmarthen-Penzance	2	55
6.51		1.45 Bristol-Falmouth	4	17
6.14		4.40 Paignton-Bristol	3	40
8.35		9.15 Liverpool-Plymouth	5	37
6.20		8.6 Sheffield-Kingswear	3	2
4.6	P	9.30 Paddington-Newquay	-	48
7.0		5.15 Paignton-Nottingham	3	33
8.0		8.45 Liverpool-Penzance	4	19
4.45	P	10.35 Paddington-Penzance	-	13
8.11		7.0 West Hartlepool-Paignton	2	38
8.48		6.7 Plymouth-Bristol	-	59

7031 *Cromwells Castle*   83D
11.50 pm   Paddington-Penzance
11.50 am   Penzance-Paddington

1000 *County of Middlesex*   82A
5.30 pm   Glasgow-Plymouth
1.45 pm   Newquay-Paddington

1009 *County of Carmarthen*   82A
          ?Bristol-Penzance
10.45 am   Penzance-Sheffield

5983 *Henley Hall*   81C
6.55 am   Paddington-Penzance
2.35 pm   Penzance-Glasgow

5054 *Earl of Ducie*   82A
12.25 am   Manchester-Plymouth
 4.50 pm   Penzance-Manchester

4976 *Warfield Hall*   83D
9.35 am   Bristol-Penzance
P 1.20 pm   Penzance-(NA)

1025 *County of Radnor*   84G
7.0 am   Birmingham-Penzance
4.40 pm   Penzance-Bristol

5005 *Manorbier Castle*   83A
8.17 am   Carmarthen-Penzance
4.20 pm   Penzance-Newton Abbot

For notes see page 141

Return engine workings from Bristol or beyond

7029 *Clun Castle*   83A
6.50 am   Paignton-Bradford
8.6 am   Sheffield-(NA)

5005 *Manorbier Castle*   83A
7.40 am   Newton Abbot-Swansea
8.17 am   Carmarthen-(Plymouth)

6814 *Enbourne Grange*   83A
8.30 am   Paignton-Derby
7.30 am   Newcastle-Paignton

7000 *Viscount Portal*   83A
8.45 am   Kingswear-Bradford
1.45 pm   Bristol-(NA)

7903 *Foremarke Hall*   81A
9.5 am   Paignton-Manchester
3.10 pm   Manchester-Plymouth

4960 *Pyle Hall*   81D
8.5 am   Newquay-Newcastle
9.25 am   Bradford-Paignton

5011 *Tintagel Castle*   83A
12.30 pm   Paignton-Manchester
11.45 am   Manchester-Plymouth

PART THREE
1971

Introduction

Having spent a long time studying a 1957 summer Saturday, we decided to return to the scene of action in 1971, to compare the flow of traffic and punctuality of working.

The two main differences are the complete takeover by diesel locomotives, and the smaller number of passengers handled.

The North-to-West route via Shrewsbury is now only used at summer weekends. Only one route is now followed between Birmingham and Bristol: the former Midland line as far as Gloucester and the former Great Western line from Yate into Bristol via Filton Junction.

An innovation in 1971 was the daily through train between Edinburgh and Paignton, as well as some very long advertised non-stop runs on summer Saturdays. For instance the down *Cornishman* had no public stopping point between Chesterfield and Plymouth, and the 7.26 Newcastle-Paignton and the down *Devonian* were advertised non-stop from Sheffield to Taunton.

By 1957 the seat regulation scheme had been extended to all departures from the Torquay branch from 6.35 am until late afternoon, and certain trains from Newquay. In 1971 it covered all trains in either direction whether for Paignton or Penzance until mid-afternoon, the only exception being down trains originating at Liverpool. Seats now have to be reserved for long-distance journeys, and an extra fee is charged for Paddington trains. Loadings are reduced compared with the 1950s, but trains of 13 and 14 coaches can still be seen.

Newton Abbot and St Austell are Motorail terminals, and in 1971 there were seventeen different Motorail services operating to the West of England, of which nine feature on a Saturday. These consist of complete train-loads between Kensington and St Austell, and between Newton Abbot and Stirling, Sheffield and Sutton Coldfield. Motor-car vans are attached to passenger services between Worcester and St Austell, Worcester and Newton Abbot, Cardiff and Plymouth, and Bristol and Newton Abbot. The Bristol vans are conveyed by a down Leeds-Paignton train and an up Paignton-Nottingham train. Finally there is the hybrid 8.30 Kensington-Newton Abbot Motorail and 16.45 return, which is combined with the 8.42 Ealing Broadway-Paignton passenger train and 16.20 return.

Four types of express passenger locomotive work in the West of England at present, together with an occasional Hymek Class 35. The 'Warships' are on the decrease; the mainstays are the 'Western' Class 52, 'Brush' Class 47, and 'Peak' Classes 45 and 46.

Locomotives from the Eastern and London Midland Regions work through to the West of England more and more each year, un-like in steam days when there was a virtual iron curtain at Bristol. Inter-regional trains to Cornwall normally change engines at Plymouth, but Paddington departures now work through un-changed to Penzance, as none of the diesel types is restricted from crossing the Saltash Bridge.

But stops for crew-changing have become more frequent. In 1971 Paddington to Exeter was the longest distance worked by a single crew, and numerous stops were scheduled for crew-changing at Taunton and Exeter. On the other hand, as will be seen, many more Cornish trains pass non-stop through Newton Abbot.

Almost the whole of the area under review is still controlled by the block system of signalling, but the number of signalboxes is greatly reduced compared with 1957. Between Taunton and Exeter (30.8 miles) there are now 8 intermediate signalboxes, and 5 between Exeter and Newton Abbot (20 miles); in 1957 there were 19 and 12 respectively. Thus the general headway of trains between Taunton and Exeter has been reduced from 6-8 minutes in the 1950s to 10-12 minutes in 1971. Diesel locomotives are far quicker to recover from checks, and it will be seen how the cumu-lative effect of delays was reduced in 1971 compared with 1957; but the longer block sections can also cause delays to Paddington trains between Reading and Taunton, one section (Castle Cary to Somerton) being just over ten miles long.

At Bristol the St Philips Marsh avoiding line is no longer used, and all trains changing engines or remanning are scheduled to do so in Temple Meads station. Only one train, the 8.45 Kingswear-Cardiff, was actually booked to pass Temple Meads without stop-ping. However, our observers saw a number of trains pass non-stop, and a train passing on the through line at up to 40 mph is something Temple Meads had never seen before 1971. It was subsequently discovered that in both directions trains were stopping to change crews before they reached the station, down trains at Dr Day's Bridge Junction and up trains at Bristol West.

The layout at Cogload has changed little. At Taunton the main line platforms were closed some years ago but in 1971 were given numbers again and are available for emergency use subject to removal of a temporary cover across the top of the stairway. From our survey it would appear that the kind of emergency envisaged is a more long-term one than the exigencies of summer Saturday traffic.

West of Taunton the relief line exists as far as Silkmill Crossing but in practice passenger trains are dovetailed into one stream at Taunton West Box, thus partially restoring the layout that existed before 1932. Three intermediate signalboxes have been closed between Silkmill and Wellington, a distance of nearly six miles. This long block section, coming immediately after the Taunton bottleneck, really governs the headway of down trains over the whole section to Newton Abbot, and causes the only substantial delays to traffic nowadays.

Exeter St David's is still the busiest station in the West Country, although the pattern of operations has changed somewhat since the 1950s. There is hardly any overtaking of main line trains on a summer Saturday. With the increased headway between trains, and shorter station stops, expresses can now stop at Exeter and proceed without delaying one another. In the down direction most advertised non-stop trains are booked to stop on the through line to change crews, while the up relief platform, even on summer Saturdays, is used by the roughly two-hourly departures for Barnstaple. Another two-hourly service, the Okehampton multiple-unit using the erstwhile Exe Valley bay, completes the total of passenger traffic over the former SR line to North Devon. So it is the central island platforms 3 and 4 that have seen the biggest change, having lost all their through express traffic with the sole exception of the Barnstaple Junction-Paddington train. The Waterloo trains all terminate here and in most cases the stock is cleaned in the platform and returns to Waterloo about an hour later. Similarly the Brighton-Plymouth train in 1971 went no further than Exeter St David's.

Newton Abbot has changed a great deal since the 1950s. The layout has only been slightly simplified, and also altered to suit the Motorail traffic. But there is a complete absence of scheduled engine changing, and pilot engines are no longer needed on the

South Devon banks. One of the main causes of delay to traffic in 1957 has thereby been eliminated.

Down Trains

The 1971 survey was carried out on Saturday 24 July. The weather consisted of sunny periods with some heavy rain. We had observers at Reading General, Bristol Temple Meads, Taunton, Exeter St David's and Newton Abbot. During the 24 hours from midnight to midnight 6 additional trains were due to arrive in the West of England, compared with 35 on 27 July 1957. Three of the extra trains ran overnight, so that between midnight and 7.00 27 down trains were scheduled to pass Whiteball summit, an average of one every 15½ minutes, compared with one every 8¾ minutes in 1957.

In 1971 therefore there was little likelihood of any very late running by the overnight trains; apart from the Stirling Motorail the last of these passed Newton Abbot about 8.00.

The 9.45 Cardiff-Penzance caused the first major delay to down traffic. Hauled by 1656, and including two Motorail vans for Plymouth, this train stopped on the up through line at Temple Meads to reman and departed 18 minutes late. The headcode, 8C04, suggests that there had already been a failure or last minute substitution. It may have been overtaken by the 7.30 Leicester-Paignton which passed non-stop on the down through, but the Cardiff's arrival time at Bristol is not known.

The Leicester train, advertised non-stop from Birmingham to Dawlish, stopped on the down main at Taunton at 11.35, 11 minutes early, to allow the 8.30 Kensington-Paignton to depart first. Then the 9.45 Cardiff was given the road through Taunton on the relief line ahead of the Leicester. But the Cardiff made an unscheduled stop, and in under two minutes 1656 attempted to restart but was unable to do so, apparently because of a faulty cooling system. The 7.30 Leicester then departed, and had a clear run to Exeter.

D7040 was called from the shed to remove 1656 and take over the 9.45 Cardiff from Taunton. The Cardiff left at 12.18 after a wait of 35 minutes, and regained time as far as Newton Abbot, where the 7.56 Wolverhampton-Penzance had already made a special stop for Plymouth line passengers. When the Cardiff train reached Newton Abbot D7040 required a pilot, a request for which Newton Abbot is no longer ready these days, and there was a further wait of 22 minutes while 813 *Diadem* was brought from shed and attached. During this time the 9.52 Paddington-Newquay passed through platforms 1 and 2, an unusual route for a Plymouth line non-stop. The 9.45 Cardiff's departure was 63 minutes late, not quite the worst of the day.

Meanwhile back at Taunton the 9.30 Paddington-Paignton had been held outside waiting for the 9.45 Cardiff to leave. If the 9.30 had been on time, there might have been occasion to open the down main platform, and allow the 9.30 to call and depart at its public time of 11.58 (10 minutes early by the working book), so that the non-stop 9.52 Paddington-Newquay could follow and also overtake the Cardiff. But the 9.30 Paddington had itself suffered an engine failure at Reading, where 841 *Roebuck* had to be replaced by 1666 *Odin*, leaving 19 minutes late. This locomotive kept time as far as Taunton East, where the 9.30 was stopped on the relief line for at least 5 minutes, and eventually entered the platform under calling-on signal behind the Cardiff, the first of seven trains to enter Taunton in this manner in the next three hours.

The 9.52 Paddington, with distant signals off, passed the crowded 11.10 Bristol-Taunton multiple unit outside Taunton, as well as the 9.30 Paddington in the station as scheduled: the 11.10 Bristol entered the platform while the tail of the 9.30, held at Taunton West, still obstructed the far end.

The 9.52 and 9.30 each lost 6 minutes to Exeter; when the 10.15 Paddington-Paignton reached Taunton there was a blank pathway ahead, the Bristol DMU having terminated, and so the 10.15 got through to Newton Abbot with little further loss of time.

The following *Cornish Riviera Limited* did not keep up with the 10.15, and took 41 minutes from Taunton to Exeter against a schedule of 29. The *Limited* was severely checked at Taunton West and, in the light of later happenings, it is possible that D1009 *Western Invader* had trouble climbing Wellington bank.

As the congestion caused by the 9.45 Cardiff was beginning to ease, another failure, this time at Exeter, made conditions even worse during the busy lunchtime period. The 9.48 Birmingham-Paignton was introduced in 1971 to compensate for the long non-stop runs made by certain trains from the North. Hauled by 1688, it passed Temple Meads non-stop, but was stopped by signals at Bristol West to give precedence to a late running train for

Weston-super-Mare. It was stopped again outside Taunton by the 10.15 Paddington; and, having reached Taunton in front of the *Limited*, was held 4 minutes over time to allow the latter to pass; departed, and was immediately pulled up at Taunton West starter for 5½ minutes, during which time the 8.23 Nottingham-Paignton entered the platform behind it.

When the 9.48 Birmingham eventually reached Exeter 21 minutes late at 13.31, 1688 had overheated and had to be taken off. 1926 was on the banker spur, having worked in much earlier on the 6.52 Salisbury, and replaced 1688 so quickly that the total wait was only 13½ minutes.

But the result of this happening on top of the existing delays was that over the next hour 6 following trains, including the *Cornishman,* lost 83 minutes between Taunton and Exeter, an average of 13.8 minutes each. The worst was the 9.25 Derby-Penzance, which took 50 minutes against a schedule of 32 pass-to-stop.

Then yet a third locomotive mishap occurred during the busiest period of the day, The *Limited* had unaccountably lost a further 3 minutes between Exeter and Newton Abbot, and passed there 15 minutes after the departure of the double-headed 9.45 Cardiff-Penzance. What happened next is not known for certain, but from the evidence available it can fairly be presumed that D1009 stalled on Dainton bank, and that a Class 47 was sent from Newton Abbot to assist in the rear.

The next three Plymouth line trains after the *Limited* were stopped at Newton Abbot for 10-16 minutes, and an apology was made for delay caused by 'the failure of a preceding train'. 1638, the locomotive off the Stirling train, was despatched light in a westerly direction from Newton Abbot and returned at 14.54, 57 minutes after the *Limited* had passed through.

The 9.25 Derby-Penzance was stopped in platforms 3 and 4 at Newton Abbot, and before it left the *Cornishman*, 7.00 Bradford-Penzance, arrived on the down through line and waited 15½ minutes.

The following 11.20 Paddington-Penzance spent 5½ minutes on the through road at Exeter remanning, and a late-running multiple-unit from Exmouth was given precedence at the west crossover. Meanwhile the 7.50 Leeds-Paignton, consisting of 14 coaches and

2 Motorail vans from Bristol, stopped in platform 1, and departed only 3 minutes after the 11.20. This close running caused a build up between Exeter and Newton Abbot for the next hour, in which 7 trains, including the Leeds, lost 57 minutes, an average of 8.1 minutes each.

The 11.20 Paddington stopped in platforms 3 and 4 at Newton Abbot, after the 9.25 Derby had left. During its 16 minute stay the 7.50 Leeds arrived in the other platform, and overtook after detaching its two vans. Thus both down platforms at Newton Abbot were occupied simultaneously for 6 minutes.

From 14.00 onwards schedules were mainly kept between Taunton and Exeter, and a gradual recovery began throughout the area. The 7.26 Newcastle-Paignton was the first train to reach Taunton on time, and the 13.10 Cardiff-Paignton was the first to keep time right through to Newton Abbot. The next three trains, from Liverpool, Manchester and London, also kept time.

Towards the end of the afternoon, when the rain had blown over and the evening was set fair, a third engine failure occurred on the down line to disrupt the progress of the remaining arrivals.

The 13.00 Birmingham-Plymouth relief, hauled by 116, left Bristol at 14.54½, and is reported to have failed at Bridgwater. D1041 *Western Prince* was at Taunton, having arrived there at 14.13 on a freight train, thought to be the 3.25 Etruria clay empties. D1041 was despatched from Taunton at 15.51 and reappeared just under an hour later hauling the failed 116 and its train, by now 70 minutes late.

During this time a special railcar was despatched from Exeter to Paignton, to fill what would otherwise have been a gap of over an hour.

D1041 took just under ten minutes to remove the failure at Taunton, back on to the train and depart, and from then on 11 minutes were made up to Newton Abbot, the time of 20¾ minutes from Exeter to Newton Abbot being the fastest of the day.

The effect of the failure was that four trains following on the Bristol line, including the *Devonian,* reached Taunton between 62 and 25 minutes late. The 14.30 Paddington-Penzance should have got by unscathed, but it too had suffered a failure at Reading, where 842 *Royal Oak* had to be removed owing to continual water and oil tripouts. The replacement, D1824 of the Birmingham Division, left Reading 21 minutes late, and must have passed Cogload after the *Devonian.* So after the Birmingham relief five trains arrived at Taunton in the space of half an hour. However, the volume of traffic at this time was not sufficient for any reaction to be felt west of Taunton, and the greatest delay between Taunton and Exeter was only 2 minutes.

Up Trains

On 24 July 1971, 49 up trains were scheduled to depart or pass Newton Abbot between 7.00 and 17.00, an average of one every 12¼ minutes, compared with 63 trains in 1957.

Punctuality was better in the morning than the afternoon. Between 7.30 and 13.00 27 long distance trains left Newton Abbot, of which 23 were on time or early, and the maximum lateness was 2 minutes. 24 of these trains were seen at Taunton, where 14 were on time or early, and the maximum lateness was 4 minutes.

From lunchtime onwards timekeeping in general deteriorated. 852 *Tenacious* failed at Newton Abbot with the 12.25 Paignton-Worcester and had to be replaced by 806 *Cambrian*; this took 18½ minutes, during which time the *Cornishman* went by. With a margin of 27 minutes behind the previous train 136 on the 13-coach *Cornishman,* 9.50 Penzance-Bradford, covered the distance from Newton Abbot to Exeter in 19½ minutes — a rare feat to average less than even time over this difficult section — but slackened off somewhat after Exeter. The Worcester train, following the *Cornishman,* did well with its new engine and made up time steadily to Taunton. Here it was able to cut its scheduled wait of 14 minutes (for the *Cornishman* to overtake) by more than half, and so departed on time having cancelled out a 15 minute late departure from Newton Abbot.

The 10.25 Newquay-Paddington covered the 137¾ miles from Exeter to Reading in 114½ minutes, and trains ran mainly to time for the next hour.

Then just as the carflats were being attached to the passenger coaches of the 14.15 Sutton Coldfield Motorail at Newton Abbot, some brake trouble was discovered on one of the empty carflats. This took half an hour to repair, during which time two Paddington trains overtook, and the Motorail departed 26 minutes late at 14.41. Such out of course running delayed the next three trains, especially the 11.50 Newquay-Nottingham, which followed the Motorail and lost 12 minutes between Newton Abbot and Bristol.

Traffic was thinning out at Newton Abbot from 16.00 onwards, but for the next two hours trains from the Plymouth line appeared 15-20 minutes late, and the 16.15 Plymouth-Cardiff was as much as 45 minutes behind time. It subsequently emerged that the loco-motive on the 13.45 Penzance-Paddington had failed at St Erth owing to lack of coolant. This train was due to wait at Plymouth from 15.55 to 16.30, thus providing a connection from Cornwall into the 16.15 to Cardiff. When the 13.45 Penzance eventually reached Plymouth it was allowed to leave before the Cardiff train.

Comparison with 1957

In 1971 there were 35 down trains scheduled to pass Whiteball summit between 10.00 and 16.00, at an average headway of 10¼ minutes. The usual allowance between Taunton and Exeter was 32-35 minutes, but 7 trains during the day covered the distance in less than 30 minutes, all start-to-stop.

During the busy mid-day period, with 18 trains arriving in the area in 3 hours, the position can only be described as critical: an engine failure at Taunton, after which only four more trains got through before one failed at Exeter, and on top of that the one in front of the Exeter failure was in trouble beyond Newton Abbot. Yet the longest time taken between Taunton and Exeter was 50 minutes, and only 4 trains took more than 45. The greatest loss on schedule between these points was 18 minutes.

In 1957 48 trains were booked to pass Whiteball between 10.00 and 16.00 at an average headway of 7½ minutes, and although so far as is known there was no failure or incident of any other kind, the only available figures for comparison show that at lunchtime trains were taking 100-120 minutes between Taunton and Exeter, and in the evening a train was still taking just under two hours.

Because of the loss of traffic since the 1950s it has never been possible to compare conditions with all-steam and all-diesel haul-age. The difference in margins between 1957 and 1971 is perhaps crucial in operating this section. As for motive power, not only are diesel locomotives mechanically more efficient at starting from checks (especially with the rather lighter loads of 1971), but there must have been little encouragement for the crew of a steam engine to make a quick start from a signal check when they were certain there would be another a few miles on.

The difference in the number of trains that can be handled between Taunton and Exeter is very marked: in 1957 there were 13 at one time around mid-day, while the most in 1971 was 6. But from this survey one is led to conclude that this factor does not have a significant effect between Taunton and Newton Abbot in heavy traffic.

The timings between Exeter and Newton Abbot show the same story. In 1957 every train from 11.10 to 16.40 took an hour or more, and the worst time for a train without intermediate stops was 80 minutes. In 1971 the worst time, including trains stopping intermediately, was 42½ minutes, and between 14.00 and 15.30 trains were often block-and-block, ie 5 trains between Exeter and Newton Abbot. In 1957 there were 9 or 10 trains in this section for most of the afternoon.

A major cause of delay in 1957 was the time taken to deal with trains at Newton Abbot. Now that there are no longer any scheduled engine changes nor pilots to be attached, the comparative figures for station time are very revealing. In 1957 44 down trains had to be dealt with between 10.30 and 16.30; in 1971 there were only 23, the remainder passing non-stop. The 44 trains in 1957 spent an average of 10½ minutes at Newton Abbot; the average of the 23 in 1971 was only 5¾ minutes.

In 1971 there were only five occasions during the whole day when Newton Abbot's two down platforms were occupied simultaneously. In 1957 this was happening continually, so that in the event of a delay the next train, if making a passenger stop, would be held up; on 27 July down trains were actually timed to overlap in many instances.

As for the Torquay branch, the layout at Paignton is no less confined now than in 1957. In 1971 the frequency of departures eased off after 14.30, and arrivals at Paignton from this time onwards were despatched back to Newton Abbot as soon as possible, train engine and all, either as empty stock or in the form of a local service. The patrons of the 18.25 Paignton-Newton Abbot, for example, must have been impressed by their 12-coach train.

Study of the up working is not of such interest, since the dates in question were at the beginning of the main holiday fortnight, and were by no means peak Saturdays for return travel.

In 1957 the delays to up traffic stemmed from two main causes: late starts, chiefly from Paignton, owing to the late running of down trains; and slow progress by certain trains up the steady climb from Exeter to Whiteball.

On 24 July 1971, although one down overnight train was seen at Newton Abbot more than half an hour late, the volume of traffic was so reduced compared with 1957 that it was unlikely that late running of down trains would react on up departures. In fact the last overnight train to Paignton passed Newton Abbot at approximately 8.00, and there were only two departures from Paignton before 8.00. The early departures from the branch all got away on time, and no up branch train reached Newton Abbot more than 1 minute late until after 14.00.

On the Exeter-Taunton section the majority of trains kept time, and no less than 26 covered the distance in better than even time — 30 minutes or less. The fastest time was 26 minutes by three trains, two of them start-to-stop, at an average of 71 mph.

Locomotives

Locomotives recorded on express passenger duty on the West of
England main line on 24 July 1971:

1. Summary of locomotive types

Western Class 52	:	23	
Brush Class 47	:	37	(3 failure
Peak Class 46	:	9	
Peak Class 45	:	15	(1 failure
Warship Class 43	:	6	(3 failure
Warship Class 42	:	4	
Hymek Class 35	:	2	

2. 'Foreign' locomotives

    London Midland Region

D02 Birmingham Division	:	8
D05 Stoke-on-Trent Division	:	2
D16 Nottingham Division	:	15

    Eastern Region (S)

40B Immingham	:	2

    Eastern Region (N)

52A Gateshead	:	4
55A Leeds (Holbeck)	:	5

APPENDIX
Table

Schedule showing progress of trains to and from
West of England 27 July 1957

Notes

Each column shows actual time and number of minutes late.

An asterisk denotes an approximate time (mainly at Exeter).

Two asterisks mean very approximate.

Capital letters in the columns indicate a train booked to call at stations within a section:

TJ	Tiverton Junction
St T	Exeter St Thomas
SX	Starcross
DW	Dawlish Warren
D	Dawlish
T	Teignmouth

Brackets round a reporting number denote number allocated but not carried.

Other notes:

AE	Stop for assisting engine
E	Early
ECS	Empty coaching stock
EXE	Exeter
LE	Light engine
NA	Newton Abbot
P	Pilot engine
Q	Runs when required
R	Engine running in reverse
RT	Right time
V	Vans
W	Stop for water

Down Trains

Train	10.25 Wolverhampton Paignton	10.0 Nottingham Paignton	11.23 Coventry Paignton	10.40 Wolverhampton Paignton	11.45 Paddington? Penzance	10.20 Sheffield Paignton	12.25 Birmingham (New Street) Paignton	11.10 Manchester? Penzance	11.37 Derby Paignton	8.15 Keighley Paignton	11.50 Paddington Penzance
Reporting No	807	410	409	808	-	413	414	-	421	422	016
Load	-	-	-	-		-	-		-	10	9+2V
Loco to NA										1024	7031
from Plymouth										1024	6813 & 7031
Taunton											
Wellington											
Exeter											
Dawlish	6.13 112 T	6.22 85 T	6.29 72	6.41 116 T	6.47 63	7.09 93	7.29 113	7.36 42	7.41/7.43 111/111 T	7.49 103	7.53/7.57 107/108 T
Newton Abbot										8.24/8.36 122/128	8.38/8.47 130/131
Plymouth											

Train	8.45 Bradford Paignton	10.30 Manchester (Vic.) Paignton	5.30 Glasgow Plymouth	10.45 Rotherham Paignton	10.10 Hull Paignton	8.00 Exeter Kingswear	11.10 Manchester Paignton	9.32 Newton Abbot Paignton
Reporting No.	415	258	214	412	417	-	230	4?
Load	10	14 to NA 10 from NA	12	9	10	4		
Loco to NA	7034	5078	1000	6954	6957	5038	5986	5011R
from NA	6962R	4983R	1000	6954	6904R	5038	5986	-
from Plymouth	-	-	-	-	-	-	-	-
Taunton								
Wellington								
Exeter		8.15 T 82				All stns.		
Dawlish	8.3/8.7 104/105 T		8.20/8.23 99/99 T	8.28/8.31 116/117 T	8.36/8.40 82/81 T			
Newton Abbot	8.40/8.57 120/129	8.51/9.7 102/112	9.2/9.10 120/120	9.13/9.21 142/145	9.20/9.50 99/120	9.24/9.31 36/35	9.36/9.42 104/97	/9.55 /23
Plymouth								

Train	9.5 Newcastle Paignton	7.20 Taunton Exeter	11.35 Liverpool Penzance	Bristol? Penzance	6.5 Cardiff Paignton	10.50 ECS Newton Abbot Torquay	9.30 Exeter Kingswear
Reporting No	418	?	202	-	700	12	-
Load	12		15 to NA 14 from NA	7	10		9 to NA 6 from NA
Loco to NA	5027	6874	1002	1009	5067	-	3677
from NA	6863R	-			5341R	6865R	3677
from Plymouth	-	-	6856 & 1002	1009 & 5196	-	-	-
Taunton		All stns.					
Wellington							
Exeter		8.44*/ 4/	8.48*/8.56* 2/RT	9.0* /9.6*	9.21*/9.27* RT/RT		/9.32*
Dawlish	DT				T		All stns.
Newton Abbot	9.47/10.2 98/104		9.55/10.6 30/32	10.7/10.21	10.15/10.26 17/22	/10.50 RT	10.47/11.11 27/39
Plymouth							

Train	6.55 Bristol Exeter	6.55 Paddington Penzance	7.55 parcels Cardiff ? Plymouth
Reporting No	-	102	15V (leaving NA)
Load	6369	10	3850
Loco to NA from NA	-	5983	3850
from Plymouth	-	7814 & 5983	-
Taunton	All stns.		
Wellington			
Exeter	10.5*/ 13/	10.21* 15	/10.33* /576
Dawlish		10.47 27	
Newton Abbot		10.58/11.2 27/27	12.46/1.48 679/713
Plymouth			3.27/ 753/

Train	Swindon Penzance 7.00	Kidderminster Paignton 6.10	Paddington Newton Abbot 7.0	Manchester Paignton 12.8	Paddington Kingswear 7.5	Birmingham (Moor Street) Paignton 5.30	Paddington Paignton 7.40
Reporting No	420	835	103	268	101	096	108
Load	13	12	8	13 to NA 8 from NA	13	10	11
Loco to NA	6824	6950	5019	5968	7025	4988	6879
from NA	7813 & 6824	6950	-	4150	6957	4988	5959R
from Plymouth	Hall & 5356	-	-	-	-	-	-
Taunton							
Wellington							
Exeter	10.37*/10.44* 37/34	10.42* 28	10.57*/11.1* 37/41	11.6*/11.13* 166/166	11.11* 45/40	11.16*/11.22* 43/45	11.20* 35
Dawlish	11.20/11.24 T 54/56	11.6 33	11.30/11.31 52/51	11.59/12.1 T 196/196	11.45/11.52 T 58/62		12.9 69
Newton Abbot	11.52/12.0 68/70	11.16/11.25 24/27	11.56/ 59/	12.18/12.31 195/198	12.11/12.20 64/66	12.32/12.41 81/82	12.25/12.37 72/73
Totnes	12.16½ 71						
Brent	12.31/12.36 72/74						
Plymouth	1.3/1.27 73/87						

147

	Coventry Paignton 5.20	Newport Paignton 8.10	Bristol Penzance 9.35	Manchester Plymouth 12.25	Bristol Penzance 9.40	LE NA Paignton	Newton Abbot Plymouth 12.30
Reporting No	427	703	425	(262)	426	567	
Load	10	13	10	8+2V to NA 6+2V from NA	10	-	3+Vans
Loco to NA	6391	5921	7018	5054	4976	5939	7300
from NA	6391	5078R	7034 & 7018	5054	7812 & 4976	-	-
from Plymouth	-	-	4077	-	7333	-	-
Taunton			Bristol TM /9.41 /6		Bristol TM /9.48 /8		
Wellington							
Exeter	11.28*/11.32* 51/44	11.45*/11.51* 54/55	11.49* 48	12.2*/12.10* 182/181	12.7* 58		
Dawlish	12.20 74	12.41 88	12.34 76	12.52½ 208	12.46 83		
Newton Abbot	12.38/12.54 80/86	12.58/1.18 94/106	12.53/12.59 84/86	1.22/1.38 227/233	1.6/1.13 91/95	/1.37	
Plymouth			1.56/2.9 76/79	2.43/ 238/	2.25/2.41 93/101	/1.45 /75	By 3.15

148

Train	7.0 Birmingham Penzance, Paignton		8.23 Reading Paignton	
Reporting No	810		106	
Load	13 to NA		10	
	8 from NA			
Loco to NA from NA	1025		5950	
	1025		5950	
from Plymouth	1007		-	
Bristol SPM	/9.50	/7		
Taunton				
Wellington				
Exeter	12.25*	70	12.39*	100?
Dawlish	1.0	90		
Newton Abbot	1.44/1.52	121/123	1.52/2.3	145/150
Plymouth	3.0/3.10	120/122		

Train	8.5 Cardiff Kingswear	7.20 Birmingham (New Street) Paignton	6.45 West Bromwich Newton Abbot	8.10 Paddington Paignton	6.30 Wolverhampton Paignton	8.25 Paddington Penzance	6.35 Walsall Kingswear from Exeter
Reporting No	704	428	813	110	814	114	430
Load	13 to NA 10 from NA	11	?	11	12	13	12 to NA 10 from NA 70024N
Loco to NA from NA	6915 6915	6819 6819	6807	7916 5067R & 5027R	5976 5976	5055 4900 & 5055	5178
from Plymouth		-	-	-	-	7816 & 6870	N6874 pilot
Cardiff	/8.6 /1						
Severn Tunnel Jct.	8.47/8.54 7/13						
Filton Jct.	/9.18 /18						
Bristol TM	9.37/9.51 22/4	/10.7 /9					/10.25 /10
Taunton							
Wellington							
Exeter	12.48*/1.0* 89/94	1.10* 91	1.18*/1.25* 89/89	1.24* 100	1.30*/1.37* 89/91	1.35* 101	1.45*/1.50* 90/90
Dawlish	DT	T	2.7 112	T	2.19 T 117	2.16 124	2.27 T 111
Newton Abbot	2.23/2.31 142/143	2.10/2.23 116/125	2.46/3.5 ECS 138/	2.30/2.41 130/134	3.5/3.13 149/151	2.52/2.59 148/150	3.18/3.28 147/150
Plymouth						4.6/4.17 153?/152?	

Train	7.30 Birmingham (Moor Street) Paignton	6.55 Wolverhampton Paignton	7.25 Ealing Broadway Penzance	7.30 Paddington Kingswear	8.50 Paddington Paignton	6.40 Leicester Paignton
Reporting No	812	815	105	107	117	433
Load	10	13	12 (10 from Plymouth)	12 to NA 9 from NA	14	7
Loco to NA	6872	5991	5987	7901	6015	6997
from NA	6872	5991	5019 & 5987	7901	5934R & 6904R	6997
from Plymouth	-	-	6800	-	-	-
	Bristol S.P.M. /10.4 /15E	Bristol S.P.M. /10.31 /3E	Theale 9.36 60?	Bristol T.M. /10.47 /7 Yatton 11.11½ Bleadon & Uphill 11.32 Bridgwater 11.54/11.57 18/19	Theale 9.49 12	
Taunton			12.22* 98	12.22/ 28/	12.30 51	/12.44 /38
Wellington						
Exeter	1.55*/1.57 106/104	2.7*/2.10 89/86	2.15*/2.21 167/168	2.26*/2.30 99/98 SX	2.33*/2.40 126/126	2.43*/2.46 110/106 St T
Dawlish	D	T	2.50 177 T	3.19/3.23 127/129 T	?/3.33 /160 T	DW D T
Newton Abbot	3.21/3.30 155/157	3.35/3.46 133/138	3.38/3.52 210/218	3.54/4.14 143/158	3.57/4.12 167/174	4.17/4.27 154/156
Plymouth			4.45/4.55 218?/214?			

Train	9.30 Paddington Newquay	12.15 Taunton Exeter	9.35 Paddington Minehead	9.40 Paddington Paignton	10.20 Paddington Kingswear	10.30 Paddington St Ives	10.37 Cardiff Paignton	10.35 Paddington Penzance
Reporting No	122	-	123	125	128	130	706	133
Load	13	-	11	12	11	14	11	14
Loco to NA	6018	4174	4979	5933	7910	6026	7811	6025
from NA	70024 & 6018	-	-	5933	7910	4931 & 7809	7811	6026 & 6025
from Plymouth	7909 & 4906	-	-	-	-	4931 & 7809	-	7823 & 5969
	Theale 10.24 7		Theale 10.32 10	Theale 10.36 7	Theale 11.10 2	Theale 11.20 3		Theale 11.27 4
						Fairwood Jct. 12.23 11		
Taunton	12.53 51	/1.5 /50						
Wellington		2.3/? 98/ Stopping Train 2.58/ 100/		2.11 102	2.18 80	2.28 80	2.36 74	2.48 90
Exeter	2.36 115			3.1 125	3.7 102	3.14 100	3.22*/3.27 91/84	3.26 100
Dawlish	3.13 136			3.43 146	4.0 136	4.10 140		
Newton Abbot	3.46/4.6 150/166			4.19/4.29 162/163	4.24 149	4.32/4.37 152/150	4.47/4.53 134/133	4.40/4.45 148/148
Plymouth	5.10/5.23 173/177					5.32 152		5.46/5.57 156/158

Train	10.40 Paddington Paignton	9.5 Swansea Kingswear	11.5 Paddington Penzance	7.43 Nottingham Plymouth	9.31 Birmingham Penzance	8.17 Carmarthen Penzance	8.55 Wolverhampton Penzance
Reporting No	135	705	140	435	821	708	820
Load	9	10	13	13	11	12	13
Loco to NA from NA from Plymouth	5973 6879 R	5981 5981	5916 7905 & 5916	7907 4988 & 7907	6830 6848 & 6830	5005 7916 & 5005	4092 5921 & 4092
	–	–	Paddington 11.21 16 Theale 12.16 23	–			
	Paddington 10.42 2 Theale 11.33 4						
Taunton							
Wellington	2.57 90	3.4 85	3.13/? AE 76/	3.22 70	3.29 116	3.41 81	3.49 125
Exeter	3.39 104	3.43*/3.48 95/91	3.50*/3.53 85/78	4.2*/4.9 82/84	4.7 127	4.17 84	4.31 139
Dawlish		T	T	?/4.55 /111 T		?/5.7 /113 T	5.14 167
Newton Abbot	4.52/5.3 152/158	4.58/5.15 129/140	5.9/5.19 121/125	5.20/5.31 119/123	5.13/5.25 166/174	5.27/5.37 116/119	5.35/5.54 175/190
Plymouth			6.18/6.29 120/121	Laira Jct 6.40 /132	6.27/? 181/	Plympton 6.46 130	Hemerdon 6.52 204

Train	Wolverhampton Paignton 9.25	Paddington Penzance 11.0	Sheffield Kingswear 8.6	Paddington Kingswear 12.0	Paddington Plymouth 12.5	Birmingham Paignton 10.55	Wolverhampton Paignton 10.35
Reporting No	855	138	438	146	147	823	827
Load	10	14	10	13	12 to NA 9 from NA	12	11
Loco to NA from NA from Plymouth	5385 5385 -	7004 4991 & 7004 -	7029 6874 -	4098 4098 -	4919N 6860 & 4919 -	4943 4943 -	4955 4955 -
Taunton		Paddington After 11.21 Theale 12.25 38			pilot from Exeter N-6860		
Wellington	3.55 108	4.5/4.9AE 135/139	4.13/4.18 99/104	4.23/4.27 103/107	4.31/? 77/	4.41/4.44 114/117	4.50 103
Exeter	4.40 128	4.53 155	4.57*/5.5 115/113	5.1 114	5.14*/5.18 81/78 Dawlish Warren 5.45 91	5.23 126 Starcross 5.48 137	5.35*/5.40 114/113 Exminster 5.52 122
Dawlish	5.20 154	5.27 174	5.37 127	5.32 129	DT		T
Newton Abbot	5.41/5.50 163/165	5.49/6.2 183/192	6.3/6.20 141/145	5.54W/5.59W 138/143	6.12/6.25 98/105	6.19 150	6.27/6.32 129/128
Plymouth					Brent /7.7 /113?		

Train	5.45 Exeter Plymouth	1.45 Bristol Falmouth	7.45 Rotherham Paignton	8.0 Manchester Penzance Kingswear	1.25 Paddington Kingswear	1.35 Paddington Penzance
Reporting No	-	(440)	439	204	149	150
Load	6	11	9	(1. 9 from NA) (2. 5+4 from NA) 14 to NA	13 to NA 9 from NA	12
Loco to NA from NA from Plymouth	34061 34061 -	7000 6813 & 4087	5967 5967 -	7019 1. 4150 & 7019 2. 4105	4962 4962	6017 N 6926 & 6017
					Theale 2.34 16	Theale 2.45 18 N-6926 pilot from Taunton
Taunton				5.20/? AE 116/	5.25/5.29 AE 65/69 Cowley Bridge Jct. 6.9 86	5.32/? 53/ Stoke Canon 6.12 70
Wellington		4.58/5.5 119/126	5.7/5.14 124/131			
Exeter	/5.52* / 7 St Thomas /5.59 /10 All stns	5.53*/5.58* 147/146	6.4*/6.8* 150/149	6.7/6.13* 125/126	6.16*/6.20* 90/88	6.24*/6.28* 77/76
Dawlish		T		DT	DT	DT
Newton Abbot	6.38/6.44 8/6	6.42/6.51 159/161	6.50/6.57 162/162	6.58/7.43 134/172 (7.13) /137)	7.12/7.29 104/114 Aller Jct. 7.34 116	7.36/7.46 107/109
Plymouth						

Train	Liverpool Penzance Paignton 8.45	Manchester Paignton 9.0	West Hartlepool Paignton 7.0	Liverpool Plymouth Kingswear 9.15	Taunton Exeter 4.50	Bradford Paignton 9.5	Birkenhead Plymouth 9.5
Reporting No	284	212	441	(208)	-	442	216
Load	12 (7+5)	13	11	12 (8+4)	2211	12	7
Loco to NA	4963	5072	6982	4056		5922	4085
from NA	1. 1015	5072	4976 R	1. 4088		5922	4085
from Plymouth	2. 5183	-	-	2. 5195	-	-	-
Taunton					All stns		
Wellington	5.40/? 124/ Silverton 6.16 137	5.50 104 Hele & Bradninch 6.20 117	5.58 85 Cullompton 6.21 94	Burlescombe 6.29 85		Whiteball Tunnel 6.35 98	6.36 173
Exeter	6.32*/6.36* 142/142	6.38*/6.45* 126/126	6.44* 102	7.5*/7.10* 99/98	7.12*/ 78/	7.20*/7.24* 121/120	7.28*/7.37* 194/198
Dawlish	DT	DT	DT	DT		DT	SX DW D T
Newton Abbot	7.49/8.0) 173/176) /8.8) /179)	8.13/8.21 177/176	7.51/8.11 132/144	8.17/8.35) 126/(135) /8.58) /155)		8.25/8.33 146/148	8.52/8.57 231/226
Plymouth							

Train	7.30 Newcastle Paignton	3.20 Paddington Kingswear	3.30 Paddington Penzance	9.25 Bradford Paignton	7.15 Exeter Paignton	6.20 Taunton Exeter	3.50 parcels Pylle Hill Sidings Plymouth
Reporting No	444	152	153	446	-	-	-
Load Loco to NA	12	9	10	10	-	-	-
from NA	6814	5954	6029	4960	7300	5964	3840
from Plymouth	6814	5954	6029	4960	-	-	-
	-	-	-	-	-	-	-
Taunton	Norton Fitzwarren 6.37 121	Theale 4.5 2E Norton Fitzwarren 6.39 45	Theale 4.17 RT Norton Fitzwarren 6.39¼ 31	/6.25 /16 Silkmill Crossing 6.40 28		All stns	
Wellington							
Exeter	7.35* 141	7.43* 74	7.50/7.55* 71/70	8.20/8.24* 90/88	/8.27* /72	8.30*/ 63/	8.35*/9.5* 95/85
Dawlish		DT		DT	All stns		
Newton Abbot	8.39/8.47 172/173	9.13/9.27 131/135	9.3/9.6 113/116	9.18/9.33 107/113	9.31/? 89\		
Plymouth							

Train	11.45 Manchester Plymouth Kingswear	3.10 Manchester Plymouth
Reporting No	228	240
Load	5011	7903
Loco to NA from NA from Plymouth	-	Filton Jct 8.48 21
Taunton	Huntspill 7.24 48	
Wellington		
Exeter	8.55*/9.0* 68/66	
Dawlish	DT	
Newton Abbot	9.37/? 69/	
Plymouth		

Up Trains

Train	6.35 Paignton Blackburn Batley	6.50 Paignton Bradford	7.40 Newton Abbot Swansea	7.15 Paignton Paddington	7.0 Paignton Preston	8.55 Taunton Cardiff	7.0 Plymouth Paddington	7.45 Paignton Newcastle
Reporting No	568	523	570	601	239		600	533
Load	-	-	-	12	-	-	13	13
Loco to Plymouth								
to NA								
from NA	7310	7029	5005	5044	6846 & 6363	5339	6022	}6876
Plymouth								8.25/8.29 18/17
Newton Abbot								T D DW SX
Dawlish	T 7.50/7.55 37/40	T 8.0/8.4 30/32	T 8.10/8.13 12/12 DW SX St T	T 8.20/8.23 13/14	T 8.29/8.31 52/52		T 8.37/8.41 16/16	
Exeter			8.38/9.2* 7/10	8.43* 8	8.47* 51		8.55*/9.0* 14/13	9.10*/9.15* 15/15
Wellington								
Taunton	Bedminster 10.50 91	Malago Vale 10.53 58	Yatton 11.14 /30	Theale 12.14 54	Parson Street 11.0 94	Parson Street 11.3 33	Theale 12.32 63	Nailsea 11.7* 33

Train	Paignton Huncoat 8.0	Kingswear Paddington 8.0	Plymouth Paddington 7.25	Paignton Derby 8.30	Plymouth Paddington 8.30	Paignton Nottingham 8.40	Paignton Leeds 8.52	Exmouth Manchester 9.18	Ilfracombe Manchester 8.25
Reporting No	578	505	603	(546)	605	(543)	(553)	223	346
Load	12	10	4 to NA / 8 from NA	11	13	12	10		
Loco to Plymouth to NA	-	-	-	-	7814 & 6006	-	-	-	-
from NA	) 5360	) 6938	) 4707	) 6814	6006	) 4914	) 4980	) 4948	) 4704
Plymouth									
Newton Abbot / Dawlish	8.44/8.49 17/17 D	8.55 12 D	8.35/8.57 1E/9 T	9.11/9.16 16/16	9.20/9.24 2E/2E	9.20/9.27 19/21 T D	9.32 18		
Exeter	9.20* 14	9.26* 11	9.31*/9.36* 11/9	9.42* 17	9.52*/9.59* 1E/RT	10.5* 24	10.9* 23	10.4*/10.12* 9/8	
Wellington									
Taunton	Nailsea 11.7* 26	Theale 12.36 46		Uphill Jct 11.24 48		Worle Jct 11.16 23	Uphill Jct 11.20 21	Uphill Jct 11.30 18	Dunball 11.48 12

Train	Kingswear Bradford 8.45	Paignton Manchester 9.5	Penzance Manchester 6.0	Kingswear Swansea 9.5	Minehead Paddington 10.40	Teignmouth Bradford 10.15	Churston Paddington 9.45	Ilfracombe Cardiff 9.25
Reporting No	563	(579)	263	580	512	552	510	589
Load	12	11	14	10	12	?	13	?
Loco to Plymouth to NA	-	-	7813 & 4176	-	-	-	-	- -
from NA	7000	7903	1016	) 5079	4949	5919	) 5053	5345
Plymouth								
Newton Abbot	9.40/9.48 1E/2E	9.58/10.2 27/26	9.58/10.8 10/15	10.12 13			10.31 8	
Dawlish		10.18 30	10.20 14	10.27 14		10.35/10.40 14/17	10.46 10	
Exeter	10.17* 1	10.31*/10.36* 28/26	10.39* 18	10.44* 17		10.53*/10.58* 14/10	11.11* 19	
Wellington								
Taunton	Fordgate 11.59 55	Durston 12.0 65	Cogload 12.5 57	Cogload 12.9 53	Creech Jct 12.12 19 / Theale 2.0 18	Creech Jct 12.16 37	Taunton East Jct 12.21 47 / Theale 2.27 56	Taunton East Jct 12.22/ 15/

Train	Wolverhampton St Austell 7.40	Falmouth Newton Abbot 6.27	Birmingham (Moor Street) Paignton 9.43	Cardiff Paignton 10.10	Manchester Newquay 7.50	Newcastle Newquay 8.5	Kingswear Manchester 10.20	Nottingham Paignton 10.58
Reporting No	670	-	527	585	655	683	588	573
Load	13	6	9	13	15	13	13	10
Loco to Plymouth / to NA from NA	7812 & 6827) 6827	7300 -	-) 6962	-) 4983	) 4970 & 6829	4900 & 4960 / 4960	-) 6965	-) 6811
Plymouth								
Newton Abbot	10.20/10.33 2/7 T	10.37/ 7E/	10.40/10.41 33/30	10.54/11.2 23/24 T	10.59/11.5 1E/RT	11.16/11.20 RT/RT	11.24 12 T	11.34 9
Dawlish	10.55/11.0 11/14 DW		11.5 37	11.25/11.28 29/29			11.40 11	11.45 5
Exeter	11.18*/11.24* 13/13		11.23* 40	11.40*/11.45* 25/15	11.46*/11.53* 11/8	11.51* 4E	11.58* 15	12.7*/12.14* 7/1
Wellington								
Taunton	12.33 42		12.26 66	12.41 30	12.59 32		1.6 46	

Train	7.30 Penzance Bristol	8.15 Perranporth Paddington	ECS 6.20 Paignton Exminster?	10.35 Torquay Paddington	8.35 Falmouth Paddington	10.35 Paignton Wolverhampton	11.30 Torquay Paddington	11.20 Kingswear Paddington	12.45 Exeter Taunton
Reporting No	672	610	-	515	615	537	525	520	-
Load	13	12	10	11	14	13	12	13	
Loco to Plymouth / to NA / from NA	6913 & 5093 / 5093	4991 & 5043 / 5043	) 5907	) 5049	6848 & 6021 / 6021	) 6863	) 6865	) 5038	) 6820
Plymouth									
Newton Abbot	11.32/11.41 5/5	11.45/11.52 5E/2E	11.52/11.54	12.2 74	12.0/12.6 1/2	12.9/12.11 71/73	12.22 40	12.31 19	
Dawlish	11.55 6	12.5 1E		12.13 69	12.22 6	12.28 76	12.38 44	12.42½ 18	
Exeter	12.12* 7	12.22* RT	LE 12.46*/ (to shed)	12.28* 68	12.36* 5	12.50* 82	12.56* 46	1.2* 20	/1.5* /20 stopping train
Wellington		Silkmill Crossing 1.24 23		Norton Fitzwarren 1.30 95	Norton Fitzwarren 1.40 33	Norton Fitzwarren 1.50 108	Poole Siding 1.59 77	2.5 52	4.0**/ 108/
Taunton		Theale 3.15 13		Theale 3.26 91	Theale 3.32 22		Theale 4.32 98 / Paddington 5.18 90	Theale 4.15 57	

Train	12.18 Newton Abbot Paddington	11.15 Plymouth Paddington	8.20 Penzance Paddington	9.20 St Ives Paddington	12.5 Paignton Cardiff	10.0 Newquay Paddington	12.30 Paignton Manchester
Reporting No	529	620	625	630	590	638	594
Load	14	14	13	14	12	15	12
Loco to Plymouth to NA / from NA	- / 6913	6856 & 5092 / 5092	4931 & 5045 / 5045	7809 & 6027 / 6027	-) 5341)	7905 & 6000 / 6000	-) 5011)
Plymouth		Totnes ?/12.16 /6	Tigley 12.22 9	Brent 12.30 1		Bittaford 12.42 5	
Newton Abbot	ECS 11.48/12.33 /15 T	12.37/12.41 10/10	12.45/12.59 6/14	1.2 6	12.56/1.5 27/28	1.8/1.12 1/2	1.8/1.17 6/4 T D
Dawlish Exeter	12.59/1.3 22/23 1.30*/1.38* 34/31	1.36* 35	1.42*/1.48* 30/21	1.51* 31	1.55*/2.2 49/49	2.0 24	2.6*/2.10 16/10
Wellington	2.20 43	2.12 42	2.27 29	2.34 43	2.52 68	2.43 38	3.6 31
Taunton	Theale 5.12 97 Paddington 6.6 101	Theale 5.4 97	Theale 5.27 72	Theale 5.20 90 Paddington 6.24 104		Theale 5.46 101	

165

Train	Paignton Paddington 1.30	Kingswear Wolverhampton 12.15	Penzance Swansea 10.20	Newquay York 11.0	Penzance Liverpool 10.5	Plymouth Newton Abbot 12.35	Paignton Worcester 12.15 ECS	Penzance Paddington 10.0
Reporting No	530	557	663	685	285	4+2V	-	635
Load	14	13	13 (10 to Plym.)	14	11	-	12	14
Loco to NA	-	-	6837	7814 & 4075	5992 & 5196	6821	6950 R	6813 & 6008
from NA	) 5959	) 4037	) 6860 & 6812	4075	5992	-		6008
Plymouth			/1.25 /RT		?/1.2 /2	1.42/ 2/	1.34/1.40N 59	1.30 4
Newton Abbot	2.28 38	2.11/2.19 55/51 T	2.14 9E	2.3/2.9 4E/2E	1.51/1.59 3E/1			
Dawlish	2.52 50	2.40/? 54/ DW SX	2.29 6E		2.13 1			
Exeter	3.23/3.27 65/69	3.17*/3.38 64/76	2.48*/3.3 5E/RT	2.41*/2.51 RT/1	2.26 2E			2.15 19
Wellington	4.9 83	4.25 91	3.41 5	3.29 7	3.22 21			3.12 46
Taunton								Theale 5.53 85

N – Booked into Up Refuge until evening

Train	Wolverhampton Newquay 11.15	Paddington Torquay 1.55	Wolverhampton Paignton 1.55	Sheffield Penzance 10.45	Wolverhampton Penzance 11.10	Paddington Kingswear 1.40	ECS Paignton Gloucester 1.5	Paddington Newquay 12.30
Reporting No	678	540	567	688	675	535	-	640
Load	12	13	10	12	12	13	10	14
Loco to NA	7909 & 6988	-	-	6825	1015 & 5028	-	-	6858 & 7823
Plymouth to NA	4087 & 6996	)5078	)5939	7813 & 1009	4088 & 5958	)6957	4988	1015 & 5084
from NA	6996	)	)	1009	5958	)		5084
Plymouth	/1.42 /5				1.58/? RT			2.37/2.45 24/23
Newton Abbot	2.34/2.38 4/4	2.43 36	2.52 34	2.46/2.56 3/2E	2.58/3.5 4E/1E	3.7/3.11 37/33 T	3.14/3.17N 109	3.41/3.47 19/21
Dawlish		2.58 41	3.11 41	3.23 12	3.28 10	3.35/? 39/		4.10 32
Exeter	3.39 40	3.43 68	3.47 61	3.54*/4.8 27/26	4.0/4.6 28/34	4.12*/4.29 57/65		4.22 29
Wellington	4.16 47	4.32 84	4.40 85	4.53 36	4.48 45	5.17 81		5.1 37
Taunton								

N – Booked into Hackney Up Loop until evening

167

Train	Paddington Penzance 11.50	Sheffield Paignton 2.25	Paddington Paignton 2.45	Weston-s-Mare Exeter 4.5	Cardiff Newquay 12.50	Exeter Plymouth 2.30	Wolverhampton Paignton 2.55	Cardiff Kingswear 3.20	Manchester Penzance 12.0
Reporting No	645	583	545	-	655	-	577	595	205
Load	12	12	13	-	10	4	12	10 to NA 12 from NA	15
Loco to Plymouth to NA from NA	1010 7034 & 7031) 7031	) 5027	) 5067	- 6369	6305 7013) 7013	) 34061	5976 R 6954	-) 6915	6921 6988 & 6916 6916
Plymouth	2.54/3.2 16/12				3.14/3.24 15/16	/2.32 /2			3.38/4.8 8/23
Newton Abbot	3.53/3.56 7/6	4.0 71 T	4.15 64		4.15/4.17 12/14	4.6/4.20 12/15 T D Dw SX St. T.	4.45/4.52 80/82	4.59/5.7 41/43	5.1/5.15 25/31
Dawlish	4.15 10						5.7 85	5.30 T 50	
Exeter	4.26 5	4.35 75	4.43 64	/4.48 /43 All stns.	4.53*/5.0 24/23	5.5*/ 15/	5.22 82	5.45*/5.50* 49/48	5.55*/6.8* 45/45
Wellington	5.8 17	5.29 100	5.35 85	?/6.0* /47		5.52 33	5.58 87		
Taunton				6.20*/? 55/				?/6.40 /52	?/7.5 /57 Bridgwater 7.20 59 Yatton 7.43½ 59 Bristol T.M. 8.0/? 60/

Train	3.10 Paignton Wolverhampton	1.45 Newquay Paddington	1.20 Penzance Paddington	12.20 milk Penzance Kensington	4.15 Paignton Paddington	4.40 Paignton Bristol	4.32 Plymouth Exeter
Reporting No	587	647	649	-	550	(599)	-
Load	10	13	11		14	5	4
Loco to Plymouth to NA from NA	- 6872 R 5968	5023 7812 & 1000 1000	6836 4976 & 5003 5003	6809 3813	)5934 & 6904	- 5991 6391	-) 7300
Plymouth		4.24/4.30 38/35	4.29/4.38 31/28	3.51/4.40 11/21			4.35/4.42 12/10
Newton Abbot	5.12/5.24 97/104 T	5.24/5.29 34/35	5.33/5.39 30/32	5.52/5.54 11/8	5.53/6.1 73/81	6.4/6.14 59/59 All stns.	6.13/6.23 23/23 All stns.
Dawlish	5.40/5.43 103/104						
Exeter	6.3/6.6 108/100 Whiteball Tunnel 6.31 97	6.12* 43	6.20*/6.25* 45/43	6.40/6.45* 10/10	6.33* 87	7.0*/7.5* 60/55 All stns.	7.16*/ 30/
Wellington							
Taunton	6.43/6.45 97/95 Durston 6.57 99	6.52 45					
	Bristol T.M. 8.0/? 113/						

169

Train	Glasgow Penzance 2.35	Nottingham Paignton 5.15	Paddington Kingswear 4.35	Paddington Paignton 5.30	Taunton Kingswear 5.30	Newton Abbot Penzance 1.55	Paddington Millbay	Crewe Penzance 2.0 perishables
Reporting No	309	(593)	555	(558)	-	-	-	-
Load	9	9	11	9	9	6	9	9V
Loco to Plymouth	5069?	-	-	-	-	-		-
to NA	70024 & 5983	6997 R	7910	-	-	1006	) 5058	) 4084
from NA	5983	6819	7025	) 6879	) 7901	6836	)	)
Plymouth	6.36/6.42 11/17	6.28/7.0 50/77 T D	6.47/7.4 84/95 T D	7.4/7.9 71/71	7.14/7.21 51/50 All stns.	5.16/5.40 2E/RT	6.1	6.7/? 24/
Newton Abbot	7.35*/7.39* 44/43	7.44*/7.52* 85/87	7.51* 105	7.59* 87?	8.12/8.16* 48/14 All stns.	7.25/ 33/	6.59	7.49 23
Dawlish Exeter							7.25*	8.25*/8.45* 28/25
Wellington		Bristol T.M. at least 96/						
Taunton								

Train	Gloucester? Paignton 5.40 ECS	Bristol Plymouth 6.7	Exminster Paignton 4.30 ECS	Exeter Kingswear 6.30	Newton Abbot Goodrington? 6.30	Newton Abbot Penzance 4.20	Newton Abbot Taunto- 7.50 parcels & ECS	Cardiff? Paignton 8.0 ECS	Paddington Penzance 3.40 perishables	Bristol Penzance 4.40
Reporting No	-	-	-	-	-	-	-	-	-	(329)
Load	10	7 to NA 13 from NA	10	10	10	7	-	10	11V	9
Loco to Plymouth	-	-	-	-	-	-	-	-	-	-
to NA	7811 R	5023	5385	5981	4955 R	5005	-	5967	) 5028	)
from NA		4963	6856	5150		-	5981	-		) 1025
Plymouth		/6.36 /29								
Newton Abbot	7.28/8.17 83/124	7.37/8.48 32/94	7.55/8.18	8.9/8.36 47/64	8.43/ 103/	8.53/ 30/		9.2/?	9.5 25/21	9.13/9.19 16/14
Dawlish		T D		T D DW St. T.						T D
Exeter		9.25*/9.30* 94/92		9.18*/ 65/						
Wellington										
Taunton										

	6.0 ECS Kingswear Exeter?	7.20 Kingswear? Exeter	4.50 Penzance Manchester
Reporting no	-	-	-
Load	-	9	14
Loco to Plymouth			
to NA	) 4098	-	7916 & 5054
from NA	)	6874	
Plymouth	9.25		
Newton Abbot		9.30/ 81/	9.35/? 24/ T D
Dawlish			
Exeter			
Wellington			
Taunton			

Further Notes on 27 July 1957

Roger Thompson has written from Bury to say that he and his family travelled overnight from Manchester to Torquay, on the train hauled (on Western metals) by 5986 *Arbury Hall.* Although he does not recall the exact departure time, it definitely started from Manchester (London Road). The only through train from London Road to Paignton that night was the 12.8am, the other overnight services starting from Victoria. So that seems to be a conclusive answer to the query discussed on pages 82-3, and means that the 12.8am was only about half an hour late at Newton Abbot, while the 11.10pm from Victoria was nearly 4½ hours late.

We now know that the 12.45pm Exeter to Taunton local, three coaches hauled by 6820 *Kingstone Grange,* called at Wellington at 3.1pm, an hour earlier than we thought. This no doubt relieves the heavily-laden 2-6-0 on the 12.5pm Paignton to Cardiff from some of the blame for delays on the climb to Whiteball, and pages 102-6 should be read with this in mind.

The engine of the 6.35am Paignton to Blackburn and Batley was 7319 not 7310 (see page 98). And the destination of the 12.15 Kingswear in 1953 was Birmingham (Snow Hill) (see page 55). Corrections to the tables may be noted as follows. Page 144, train 230 was 12.8 Manchester (London Road) and was 33/29 minutes late at Newton Abbot. Page 146, parcels train arrived Plymouth 750 minutes late. Page 147, train 268 was 11.10 Manchester (Victoria) and minutes late should read: Exeter 243/243, Dawlish 273/271, Newton Abbot 266/266. Page 148, 9.35 Bristol to Penzance left Plymouth 81 minutes late. Page 150, 8.25 Paddington to Penzance, minutes late at Plymouth should read 152/152. Page 151, 7.25 Ealing Broadway to Penzance, delete question marks against minutes late at Theale and Plymouth. Page 154, 12.5 Paddington to Plymouth, delete question mark against minutes late at Brent. Page 160, train 568 engine was 7319. Page 164, 10.35 Torquay to Paddington was 87 minutes late at Theale; and 12.45 Exeter to Taunton load was 3, and Wellington entry should read: /3.1   /48. Page 168, 12.50 Newquay to Cardiff, reporting number should read 665, the Wellington entry 5.52, 33 should appear in column 5 referring to the 12.50 Newquay, not in column 6.

Acknowledgements

For the second half of the book our thanks are due firstly to Peter Gray, without whose expert record of Newton Abbot on 27 July 1957 nothing could have been attempted; to David Burton, Peter Tunks, Tom Reardon, Harry C. Stafford and Derek Frost for the rest of the facts on which the book is based; to S.W. Beer, Mark B. Warburton, Peter Nethercot, Michael B. Dean, Michael Hedges and D.J. Beddall for other 1957 information which has been used; to Mark B. Warburton, J.P. Simons, Stanley J. Dart, Bob Stone and Peter Gray for taking part in the comparative survey in 1971, and to James Tawse and K B Stone for other 1971 information. If anyone reading it finds that he can add anything we would be glad to hear from him.

The authors are very grateful to Kenneth Leech for photographs 1-8 and to Peter Gray for photographs 9-22.